Seasons of the Witch

AUTUMN TAROT

A journey through Mabon and Samhain

Lorriane Anderson

Illustrated by Tijana Lukovic

ROCKPOOL

A Rockpool book
PO Box 252
Summer Hill
NSW 2130
Australia

rockpoolpublishing.com
Follow us! rockpoolpublishing
Tag your images with #rockpoolpublishing

ISBN: 9781923208742

Published in 2026 by Rockpool Publishing

Cover design and typesetting by Sara Lindberg, Rockpool Publishing
Internal design by Christine Armstrong, Rockpool Publishing
Edited by Lisa Macken

Printed and bound in China
10 9 8 7 6 5 4 3 2 1

Contents

A note before you begin

This deck walks through autumn's shadows as well as its beauty. Within these cards you will find images of death, ghosts, fire, and endings. Some cards such as The Tower with its burning house portray loss and devastation, while others call you to sit with grief, transformation, or the presence of spirits.

These themes are not meant to frighten or trigger but to reflect the full truth of the season: autumn is as much about harvest as it is about release. Ghosts remind us of memory and legacy, fire of sudden change, and death of the eternal cycle of renewal. However, I acknowledge these images and ideas may be unsettling, especially if you are moving through grief, trauma, or transition. Please honor your own pace. If a card feels overwhelming you may choose to set it aside, journal about your reaction, or approach it again when you feel ready.

This deck is a companion through shadow, not a command to face what you cannot. Take only what serves you and let the rest wait until its season comes. For more ways to alter your deck to accommodate grief, trauma, or transition, please visit seasonsofthewitchoracles.com/autumntarot.

Introduction

Welcome to autumn, my darling. You hold in your hands the second of four in the *Seasons of the Witch* tarot series. Together we'll explore the 78 cards of the tarot through the lens of autumn, with themes such as death and crossing the veil, releasing and healing, shadow work and facing your fears. Each card will feel familiar but also slightly different as we incorporate interpretations that are more in alignment with fall. However, because this deck is based on the traditional Rider-Waite tarot system you can read it in the same way.

Stay open-minded as you venture through these cards. While based on Rider-Waite, you will find the imagery is significantly different in many cases. Tijana and I wanted to highlight familiar autumn symbols such as pumpkins, gnarly branches, ghosts, and eerie landscapes. I invite you to take a few moments with each card draw to explore what these autumnal symbols represent for you and add your own layers to the cards.

After having written so many decks I can honestly say that each deck pushes so much harder than I could ever have imagined at the start. I always find myself living the themes of the decks I write, and this one was no different. I found myself diving deeply into shadows and fears I hadn't needed to confront for years, especially around my capability to be a good writer with something worthwhile to say. Grief surfaced while writing more times than I care to admit, particularly regarding the death of my grandparents. Also, the need to focus on self-care and nourishment became a front and center topic in my life: most notably, how I need to take better care of my physical body instead of pushing myself to burnout.

I have said for many years that I don't write these decks, spirit does, and although that may sound clichéd it's true. I find myself experiencing the sensation of being a vessel while spirit delivers the message to me and ultimately to you, which is why I couldn't write just one tarot deck as I had originally intended. Spirit pushed and pushed for months, urging me to make four seasonal tarots even though I really didn't want to, but having just completed two of the four with this edition I understand the need to honor the seasonality of life.

We all experience seasons, and just like the sabbats those seasons do not always fit neatly inside a calendar. I wrote this deck over spring and summer but my spirit was deeply enmeshed in an autumn season. Soon I will begin work on the next deck, which I will not be writing in its season, but I have no doubt I will nevertheless experience its energy as my personal cycle.

The goal with *Seasons of the Witch*, both the oracle and tarot decks, has always been to honor the season you find yourself in. To acknowledge that you are where you are without feeling pressure to change what you're experiencing. To give yourself time to mourn as long as you need to. To feel joy even when others do not, or to rest your body instead of needing to perform productivity for a world that's forgotten how to be still.

Regardless of what season you find yourself in these tools were created to support you through it, to offer words of encouragement and resonance and to hold space for your journey, especially during those times you feel as though you're walking alone.

As always, you can use this deck in combination with the *Seasons of the Witch* oracle series, particularly Mabon and Samhain, keep it completely separate, or use it with other oracles beyond the *Seasons of the Witch* family. This deck was created to be your companion in whatever way feels most natural to you.

With my deepest gratitude,

XoXo, Lorriane ♡

The spirit of autumn

Ancestral connection
Balance
Crossroads
Death and mourning
Divination and wisdom
Embracing change and transitions
Grounding
Other realms
Planning and preparation
Protection
Self-care and nourishment
Warmth and coziness

The seasons as archetypes

An archetype is a model, prototype, or example you can follow for good or bad. It's helpful to think of an archetype as a person expressing traits or qualities you may want to emulate or avoid; for example, a healer is an archetype. Their positive qualities might be compassion, warmth, caring, and that they're a really good listener. All archetypes have shadow qualities as well, in this case the healer might play the martyr, take advantage of the pain of others by selling ineffective remedies, or use healing as a method to control people. However, if you want to step into the role of healer in your own journey you may wish to emulate the positive qualities of a healer while remaining mindful of the shadow expressions, doing what you can to avoid some of the darker natures of this archetype.

It's common to hear spiritual leaders talk about working with the "energy" of something, like the energy of fire or the energy of the zodiac sign Scorpio, but it can be challenging to understand what that energy is and how to access it. That's where archetypes come in. Fire or earth or the moon or an animal can be viewed as an archetype with positive and negative qualities to explore. The same is true for the seasons: spring, summer, fall, and winter, each of which represent expressions you can model yourself on for growth, healing, clarity, or awareness.

Tarot is a collection of 78 archetypes, with each card representing a different energy or personality. The High Priestess represents intuition and the value of learning from experience, while the Queen of Wands represents someone much like the boss woman who is confident and able to have long-term vision. These personalities come together in a reading to tell a story the same way a fairytale is created to teach children moral lessons. You'll have main characters (the major arcana) and supporting characters (the minor arcana), all interacting with each other to tell the story of where your energy is right now and where it might be heading.

The theme of a tarot deck is an additional archetype, adding one more layer of qualities to the existing ones of the tarot. What you have in your hands now is the tarot with the added layer of autumn. Remember that seasons are also archetypes, and the intention of this series of four tarots is to help you understand how the tarot's meanings can change depending on what cycle or season you're in.

Autumn represents endings, releasing, healing, and a connection with the other realms. This is the season of caring for unseen things, for turning inward and evaluating what's working in your life and letting go of what no longer serves. This is also the coziest of the seasons as it connects you deeply with your roots. Working with ancestors and familial connections is favored during the fall months, and this deck is ripe with imagery of spirits, ancestors, and the spirit realms.

How to use the cards

Cleansing your deck

Getting a new deck is an exciting moment and you're probably eager to dive right in, but before doing a reading allow yourself time and space to establish a bond with your deck and prepare it to support you. Start by cleansing your deck of any lingering energy from the handling of its creation or transportation, which will ensure your deck is coded with your energy so it becomes *yours* only without interference.

My preferred method of cleansing is with smoke, but feel free to use any method that suits you best. You may wish to consider cleansing your deck with sound, crystals, herbs, visualization techniques, or by sun or moonlight. If you decide to use smoke, I have provided a dedicated incense recipe via "Awakening the Oracle," which you can access by visiting seasonsofthewitchoracles.com/autumntarot.

Dedicating your deck

After cleansing your deck you may wish to dedicate it. To do so, find a quiet place such as in front of your altar or any place that is peaceful. Establish your ritual space by lighting incense, playing sacred sounds, drawing a protective circle if that aligns with you, and placing any additional offerings in front of you. Light three white candles and place them before you as well. Take a few deep breaths to ground and center yourself, then take an additional few breaths while holding the cards in your hands so your energy can meld with the deck's energy.

Take as long as you need to feel relaxed and engaged in this dedication ritual. Once you feel relaxed, bring the cards to your heart space and say your intentions for this deck, either out loud or to yourself. You can chant your intentions if that feels right for you, or say a prayer. Once you've set your intentions, thank the deck for holding your desires and its willingness to be in partnership with you on your divination journey. Continue holding your deck for as long as you desire, then open your eyes and close out your ritual space. Place the deck on your altar overnight, and the next day proceed to the get to know your deck spread on page 11.

Using the cards beyond autumn

The *Seasons of the Witch: Autumn Tarot* is similar to the *Seasons of the Witch* oracle series in the sense that it functions in the same way as any other tarot deck, and the meanings can apply to any situation no matter what time of year you use them. My interpretations of the cards and the images will feel the most resonant during the autumn season, but don't feel as though you can't use this tarot all year long. Your inner season may not align with the calendar, and that's okay. If you feel called to work with the *Autumn Tarot* or the themes within this deck feel in alignment for you in spring or summer or winter, then honor what your soul is yearning for.

If you aren't sure when this tarot might be right for you, consider working with it when:

- ★ you're honoring grief, loss, or the inevitability of change
- ★ you're ready to release what no longer serves you
- ★ you need clarity in murky or uncertain circumstances
- ★ you're standing at a crossroads, unsure which path to choose
- ★ you want to embody sovereignty by owning the consequences of your choices
- ★ you're facing burnout and realize you can't sustain your current pace
- ★ you're wrestling with regret or nostalgia and can't stop replaying the past
- ★ there is uncertainty in the world such as climate change, politics, or instability that makes you crave grounding
- ★ you're drawn to shadow work, exploring fears, jealousy, shame, or hidden desires
- ★ you want to ritualize the end of something, such as deleting an old dating app or journaling a farewell letter.

Combining tarot and oracle cards

Each deck, whether tarot or oracle, has a unique voice, symbolism, and energy that contributes a layer to a reading. With so many decks to choose from, it feels almost a shame to limit a reading to just one option. By adding even just one additional deck to your reading you will unlock a world of possibilities that will transform your readings into cohesive and engaging narratives that resonate on a deeper level.

The most natural combination for the *Autumn Tarot* is with either *Seasons of the Witch: Mabon Oracle* or *Seasons of the Witch: Samhain Oracle*. This tarot deck was designed to work in partnership with these two oracles to further illustrate the various energies associated with autumn. However, there is no right or wrong way to combine decks, and I encourage you to explore different ways to bring your readings to life.

Reversals

I have chosen not to include reversals in this series, but should you choose to use reversals please feel free to do so. I believe reversals aren't needed in tarot, as anything you might experience in the reverse is likely available in another card in the deck. However, should you choose to use reversals, I find it helpful to interpret them in one of two ways. The first is the direct opposite of the upright meaning; for example, the opposite of the Sunset card might be a lack of happiness, whereas the upright meaning is joy. The opposite of the Three of Autumn Swords could be healing from heartbreak, while the upright meaning typically means betrayal.

The second way I recommend reading reversals is a more stern or aggressive version of the upright meaning. For example, the Four of Pentacles represents frugality, but in the reverse it can mean it's got way out of control. The Eight of Swords represents failing to see the truth of your situation, which you may or may not be aware of. In the reverse it can mean you're intentionally choosing to avoid the truth and the harm this behavior is causing.

Ultimately, how you read tarot is up to you, and that includes how you read reversals or indeed whether you read them at all.

Card spreads

Get to know your deck spread

I have included a spread to get to know your deck in each and every single one of the *Seasons of the Witch* oracles and I still love and use that spread to this day. However, I've wanted to create a much deeper spread for a long time now, and the conception of the *Seasons of the Witch* tarots felt like the perfect time to introduce this new version. This spread will help to establish a much deeper bond and understanding of your relationship with your deck. It gives the deck space to share its voice while also uncovering why you've felt called to it in the first place. My favorite question is number 10. Giving the deck a chance to say "Don't work with me when . . ." introduces a level of respect that I felt was missing before.

- ★ **Card 1:** introduce yourself. What do I need to know about you?
- ★ **Card 2:** what's your first impression of me?
- ★ **Card 3:** what drew us together?
- ★ **Card 4:** what kind of readings can I expect from you?
- ★ **Card 5:** what's something I shouldn't expect from you?
- ★ **Card 6:** what's the most positive thing I will gain from our time together?
- ★ **Card 7:** what's one way you'll challenge me or force me to face deeper truths?
- ★ **Card 8:** what's the one card in your deck that's a mirror of who I am right now?
- ★ **Card 9:** what's the one card in your deck that's a mirror of who I am becoming?
- ★ **Card 10:** how will I know when you don't want to communicate with me?

For a more in-depth ritual for connecting with your deck, visit seasonsofthewitchoracles.com/autumntarot to gain access to "Awakening the Oracle," a 21-day guide to building an intimate relationship with your new oracle deck.

One-card draws for the autumn season

I truly believe that pulling one card a day is one of the best ways to build a bond with your deck, but as your mind, body, and soul need different things each season so might your tarot practice. Here is a list of autumn-specific questions to incorporate into your daily draws. Use them as is or as inspiration for your own autumnal questions:

★ What harvest is ready to be gathered?
★ What do you need to release?
★ How do you need to nourish yourself right now?
★ What hidden gift can be found this season?
★ What shadow do you need to face?
★ Which memory is guiding you today/this week/this month?
★ How can you create sanctuary for yourself?
★ What's transforming in your life right now?
★ How can you prepare for winter?

In recent years I have stopped using specific layouts for larger spreads, choosing to lay them out in single lines going from left to right and reading them as though they were a story. The remaining spreads offered here were created with this layout in mind.

Threshold spread

This spread was created to identify transitions and support you as you make your way from one leg of your journey to the next. Transitions aren't always obvious or sudden or occur in one singular event: oftentimes, you'll be within a transition before you begin to realize it's happening. Consider using this spread at the start and end of each season to honor the natural cycles, but also to see if you are experiencing a personal threshold that needs to be crossed.

- ★ **Card 1:** what have you outgrown and need to leave behind?
- ★ **Card 2:** what lesson or wisdom are you leaving this chapter with?
- ★ **Card 3:** what fear or resistance are you experiencing by going through this transition?
- ★ **Card 4:** how can you make the most of the liminal space between here and there?
- ★ **Card 5:** what will your new chapter look like once you cross the threshold?

Open door spread

At some point the transition must end and you'll find yourself firmly in a new chapter, and this spread is for those times. It's for when you want to be present in your current cycle and make the most of what this season has to offer. Consider using this spread at the height of each season or the beginning of each of the fixed zodiac signs: the first day of Scorpio for fall; the first day of Aquarius for winter; the first day of Taurus for spring; and the first day of Leo for summer.

★ **Card 1:** what season or cycle are you currently in?
★ **Card 2:** what opportunities or challenges will you face in this season?
★ **Card 3:** what energy or resources will this season bring?
★ **Card 4:** how will this opportunity plant seeds for the next stage of growth?

Forgotten path spread

We all have dreams we've forgotten about or parts of ourselves we've lost along the way. This spread will bring some of those buried pieces back to the surface, the ones that are important and waiting for you to be ready to resurrect them. Autumn is the perfect time to do this kind of work and I highly recommend doing it on Mabon and Samhain and then once more just before Yule. Also consider this spread when you feel a sense of yearning but can't identify the source, or when you know there's something you need to do or experience and need to find clarity.

- ★ **Card 1:** what dream or part of yourself have you lost that is waiting to be reclaimed?
- ★ **Card 2:** what pulled you away or caused you to forget?
- ★ **Card 3:** what desire or urge is being repressed while this dream/lost part remains buried?
- ★ **Card 4:** what would happen if you took steps to reclaim this dream or lost part of yourself?
- ★ **Card 5:** how can you reclaim and nourish it?

Mirror of truth spread

This spread is an easy, grounded way to begin a shadow-work journey. It invites you to confront a falsehood about yourself, rather than picking apart your brain and trying to identify it on your own. Try to make your reading space as comfortable as possible. Light scented candles, wear comfortable clothes, and even consider doing the spread on your bed or a couch where you can lie down for a few moments if anything feels too intense.

- ★ **Card 1:** what do you believe to be true about yourself?
- ★ **Card 2:** what truth is lying beneath the surface of this belief?
- ★ **Card 3:** how is this story clouding your vision?
- ★ **Card 4:** how will confronting this illusion help you move forward?

Autumnal self-care spread

Each season has its form of self-care, but autumn is most aligned with self-care overall. This spread is like a hug, showing you all the things you need to feel supported and held during the fall months. Needs can change often, so consider using this spread once a week as a part of your routine. Because self-care in tarot can feel abstract, I have created a list of self-care rituals, practices, and other resources for each of the 78 cards of the tarot that you can find by visiting seasonsofthewitchoracles.com/autumntarot.

- ★ **Card 1:** what's depleting your energy and should be avoided?
- ★ **Card 2:** what can you do to nourish your body?
- ★ **Card 3:** what will lift your spirit?
- ★ **Card 4:** what will ground your mind?
- ★ **Card 5:** how can you soothe your emotions?
- ★ **Card 6:** what will bring you the most overall comfort right now?

- ★ **Card 7:** what small action can you take to restore your strength?
- ★ **Card 8:** how can you maintain your vitality?

Descending into winter spread

This spread is meant to help you transition with grace and clarity from autumn to winter. If you live in a place where it snows, I recommend using this spread during the year's first snowfall. If, like me, you don't, then consider using this spread around the 1st of December (or 1st of June for those in the southern hemisphere).

- ★ **Card 1:** what's the first sign telling you it's time to descend into rest?
- ★ **Card 2:** what will be dormant or unavailable during your season of winter?
- ★ **Card 3:** what cannot go with you into winter?
- ★ **Card 4:** what lesson, truth, or piece of wisdom can only be revealed in silence or stillness?

Autumn
Tarot
cards

Major arcana

The major arcana consists of 22 cards, numbered in order from 0 The Fool to XXI The World, which is renamed Descending to Winter here. These cards represent the major energies you might experience in life, things such as starting a new chapter (The Fool), facing unexpected challenges (The Tower), or a need to experience more balance and moderation (Temperance). You see themes like this in the minor arcana as well, but they carry much more weight when presented as a major arcana card. Still, you will find many of these cards are mirrored within the minors, such as The Tower and Ten of Swords or The Empress and Queen of Pentacles.

Most of the names have remained the same with the exception of adding "Autumn;" however, some cards have been replaced with titles that I believe better illustrate the energy of autumn. The Magician has been replaced by The Autumn Witch because, well, this is a witch deck. Judgment has been replaced with Reckoning to eliminate religious imagery, turning the focus back on you, the reader. Justice is updated to Autumn Consequences to illustrate the cause and effect of your actions rather than strict rules and legality, and The Hanged Man is now The Autumn Hanged One to make this card more gender neutral.

The sun and the moon have been renamed Sunset and Waning Moon respectively. Like the seasons, the sun and moon move in cycles. The sun can be seen in four parts: sunrise (spring), midday (summer), sunset (autumn), and midnight (winter). Likewise, the moon appears in cycles of new moon (winter), waxing moon (spring), full moon (summer), and waning moon (autumn). This is done mostly to illustrate how joy (the sun) and illusion (the moon) may land differently with each of their phases.

0. The Autumn Fool

A maiden finds herself in a dark staircase, hidden behind a tapestry. Along the stairs are ancient tomes filled to the brim with forgotten knowledge. The stairs themselves represent the pathway into the unknown: a liminal space where a new adventure awaits her. The lantern she carries represents a promise that she will always have her own inner light to carry with her no matter how dark this path may become. The moss reminds her that life can thrive even in the most unlikely places. Moss also serves as a symbol of rebirth. She doesn't know it yet, but these are the first steps in a long journey of self-discovery and a renewed sense of life.

Divinatory meaning

It may seem like coincidence or a random occurrence that leads you on a path toward a new beginning, but that is hardly the case. A detour to work, a call from a long-lost relative, or a sudden gust of wind, as is the case with our maiden, can change the trajectory of your life. Trust that these are not mistakes, that you have been called to this journey because it's time to transition into a different version of yourself.

The Fool as a whole represents new beginnings and being brave enough (or some might say "foolish enough") to do things you've never experienced. The Autumn Fool adds another layer of complexity, urging you to descend into the darkest parts of your being to find the wealth of what lurks there. A new beginning needn't always be physical: perhaps what's changing for you now isn't something you can see, but something you're feeling within you. Grab hold of these shifts and let them stir you. Accept that you were never meant to be the same person for a lifetime, and that not only is it okay but it's encouraged to embrace fresh challenges.

The Autumn Fool is confirmation to move forward with your plans, to know that risk is a natural part of life. Every new path is a mystery and will remain so unless you're willing to learn all that it has to share.

Additional meanings for The Autumn Fool:

- trusting too quickly, revealing too much, or entering a situation without fully understanding the consequences
- hearing a soul whisper to begin something new
- an idea or instinct that won't let you go
- walking away from financial security in favor of your mental or emotional health.

I. The Autumn Witch

The Autumn Witch is her own sacred tool, drawing energy from the world around her, sure, but also from the depths of the world within her. She is a walking vessel of manifestation, having gone through the ups and downs of the year and leaving behind all things non-essential to her. She doesn't need external tools to wield her power; instead, she channels starlight, moonlight, and mist. She transmutes her pain and loss into gold. Energy moves with her and through her, dancing down from the cosmos and into the earth below. Because she is not bound by the external, all things for her are possible and she trusts that anything she wishes to call forth is already hers.

Divinatory meaning

The Autumn Witch represents a shift in the way you manifest. This is deeper, fought for, earned. It's the kind of magic that can only come from having stripped away the blocks and fears of owning your inner power. This witch calls forth energy from within, allowing herself to feel connected with the only things that truly matter: what she desires.

This is a card about confidence, about knowing you have the power and ability to control the elements of your life. When this card appears it invites you to take bold action, believing in the universe to support you in your endeavors. Now is not the time to introduce doubt into your intentions, but turn your gaze to possibilities rather than challenges. Ask yourself "How can I?" instead of declaring "I can't." Trust in your own vision rather than inviting others to comment on your plans. The Autumn Witch has summoned you to rely on two things only – yourself, and spirit – to manifest your path.

Additional meanings for The Autumn Witch:

- aligning thought, will, and action to bring ideas into form
- using skill and creativity to generate new income streams
- personal branding, charisma, or building an online presence
- claiming personal power without fear or apology.

II. The Autumn High Priestess

The high priestess stands in front of a gilded mirror representing the separation between the conscious and unconscious realms. Waves spill from the mirror's surface, symbolizing the depths of your subconscious mind, which the priestess protects. Golden pomegranate vines dance around the mirror's edge, standing as a symbol of feminine energy. Notice the priestess is half turned toward you: this is her subtle way of saying she will not seek you out but will happily let you pass through the mirror to face the deepest parts of who you are when you're ready to reach out to her. She holds a scroll in her hand to indicate her hidden knowledge.

Divinatory meaning

The Autumn High Priestess represents a key step in The Fool's journey. It isn't enough to take the leap (the fool) or to direct your intent (the witch). At some point you must look within yourself to discover the source of your desires and actions, and the urges driving your choices. This card acts as a mirror when it appears, meaning you must face what's in front of you. There's no way around your situation except to go through it, to experience it and let your inner knowing guide your path.

When you face this inner mirror you will find that it can only show you what you already know to be true. Listen to what you're feeling, and learn to trust in the signs you're sensing through your body, mind, heart, and soul. When you allow yourself to believe what you already suspect, the answers will start to fall into place.

The additional layer of autumn reminds you of the need to slow down and learn how to receive. Wisdom is revealed in the right season; there's no need to seek, only to listen. This card represents a passive energy, and when it appears it could mean trying too hard to make things make sense. Some things can only be felt rather than analyzed.

Additional meanings for The Autumn High Priestess:

- if something feels off, honoring that sense instead of brushing it away
- listening to your body's subtle cues rather than ignoring them
- recognizing unspoken dynamics at work
- allowing time for reflection instead of chasing constant input.

III. The Autumn Empress

The Autumn Empress is represented by Persephone, the queen of the underworld. She sits upon a stone throne surrounded by skulls and bones, a reminder that beauty still exists in death and decay. She holds the infamous pomegranate, the fruit that binds her to cycles of return. Wheat and poppies bloom around her, representing fall's final offering and the pause of growth.

This empress offers a different kind of nourishment, a darker, abundance-rooted gestation rather than blooming. She feeds the unseen and she's pregnant with potential, quietly tending to what's to come.

Abundance isn't born when the fields are overflowing. It begins in the shadows, in the early hours when you rise to do the unseen work or the lonely moments when your candle burns into the night. The Autumn Empress reminds you that prosperity is prepared in silence.

Divinatory meaning

I love Persephone as the vessel for The Autumn Empress. She is a goddess who is in touch with her darkness just as much as her growth. She doesn't sacrifice one for the other; rather, she nourishes each one in their respective seasons, caring for each version of herself with equal thought and consideration.

When this card appears it's to invite you to consider how you can be a support system to both yourself and others. Does something need more attention than usual? Is there a way you have not got the nourishment you require to thrive? Autumn, perhaps more than any season, is one of self-care, and receiving this card can indicate a need to make a bigger effort in tending to the various pieces of your life. This can mean traditional self-care in the form of rest and renewal. It can also mean a need to show up and nourish your community, setting boundaries, inviting more beauty into your life, or expressing yourself creatively. Take a moment now to reflect and think about what's neglected for you at this time and how you can bring renewed life to this area.

Autumn brings an additional layer of nourishing your shadows: even your darker parts need love and attention. Consider adding shadow work to your self-care routine or making time to explore your more-taboo energies.

Additional meanings for The Autumn Empress:

- creating home as a place of beauty and warmth
- prioritizing nourishment
- connecting with the archetype of the mother, earth, or great goddess
- celebrating body positivity and sensual embodiment
- slow living, homesteading, or natural wellness practices
- balancing cycles of productivity and rest.

IV. The Autumn Emperor

The Autumn Emperor is the embodiment of masculine energy in feminine form during the season of autumn. She's one with the land, sitting on a throne grown from the earth itself. She listens. She witnesses. She protects. She does so from a place of love and compassion, which is what sets her power apart. She doesn't rule with force; she rules with understanding. She still emulates the qualities of an emperor, having vision, making tough calls, and knowing how to encourage greatness in those around her, but she is also softer in autumn. She rules with an open heart and steady mind.

Divinatory meaning

The Autumn Emperor is a card of structure, authority, personal power, and discipline, but through the lens of autumn this card softens just a little. This figure is still a force to be reckoned with: cross her and she will punish accordingly, but she will do so with honesty and fairness. However, she only pushes because she can recognize your potential. She can see the ways you have not taken responsibility for the greatness lurking within you.

This card appears in a reading when you are lacking personal sovereignty, when there is a need to establish better structure within your life. You may need more discipline to set firmer boundaries and focus on your own vision rather than trying to fix someone else's, or perhaps a combination of all three.

You are your authority, you are your own emperor. It's time to start ruling your kingdom as though you're in charge of it, instead of participating as a bystander. This card invites you to question your relationship with your personal power, to understand what you need in order to feel more grounded and find stability.

Additional meanings for The Autumn Emperor:

+ leadership roles, promotions, or management positions
+ navigating authority figures, institutions, or bureaucracy
+ father figures, authority figures, or masculine archetypes shaping relationships
+ masculine health issues or those connected with bones, spine, or structure
+ conversations around patriarchy, authority, and control.

V. The Autumn High Priest

The Autumn High Priest stands beneath an arched canopy of trees, her figure veiled in white and crowned with a golden halo of radiance. She offers the promise of knowledge to the initiates surrounding her. The presence of each of these women emphasizes community, tradition, and the transfer of knowledge from teacher to student. Two apprentices nearest to the high priest hold keys, which represent both the unlocking of hidden wisdom and the responsibility that comes with holding such power. The Autumn High Priest does not simply open doors: she chooses who is ready to step through.

Divinatory meaning

The Autumn High Priest is traditionally known as The Hierophant and represents systems and established fraternities. For many years this card has been associated with rigidity, exclusivity, and religious dogma; therefore, many have felt out of alignment with its message. It's true that this card can indicate strict and uncompromising rules, but it can also appear when truths are being passed down, studied, or experienced within the grace and guidance of community, ancestry, or tradition.

This card can represent showing respect to your elders, learning the traditions of your culture, or finding resonance within a gathering of like-minded individuals. When this card appears it's to invite the question: what teachings are you inheriting, and what part of this knowledge would you like to hold for yourself?

This is not an all or nothing card: you can choose how much is right for you and what needs to be discarded. Like leaves falling to nourish the soil, certain beliefs and practices must be released to make way for deeper, personal truths that can exist within a whole.

The arrival of this card can mean your situation will greatly benefit from a mentor, teacher, or guide who can help you navigate complexities you do not yet have the skill to manage. Follow the steps presented to you in the way they were intended and then invite ways to make the situation your own. In time you will gain the knowledge and experience to decide your own path, but for now know that there is help available to you.

Additional meanings for The Autumn High Priest:

- honoring rituals, seasonal observances, or spiritual practices that root you to community and history
- navigating workplace hierarchy: either respecting authority or questioning outdated systems
- family expectations weighing on your choices in love
- formal study, certification, or initiation into a new discipline
- understanding systemic influence: how authority shapes culture, family, and personal belief.

VI. The Autumn Lovers

The honeymoon phase has been over for this couple for many moons. They're grayed and weathered, yet love for each other clearly exists in their eyes. They've stayed the course and chosen each other again and again. They've done the work over the years, especially when times were tough. They listened, they supported one another, they showed their care: not just in words, but in daily action and consistent effort. Now when all of the children are gone and the house is paid for, they choose to rest within each other's company.

Divinatory meaning

In autumn, The Autumn Lovers becomes a card of devotion. It represents commitment long after the luster wears off. In a relationship this card may appear when looks have faded and money is tight, but love remains beyond the shallowness of youth. As always, The Lovers is never just a card about love, though the appearance of this card can indicate a long-lasting connection. This card represents following your heart and values, which are what will sustain you when challenges arrive. It's what will hold you when it seems the world is directing all of its efforts into breaking you down.

What choice are you making at this moment? Are you choosing the easy path, the one that offers no obstacles or tough decisions, no need for integrity or intense thinking, or will you make the harder choice, the one that may need to be defended or protected and the path that feels most like what your heart is yearning for.

This is your invitation to open yourself up to the possibility that's whispering your name, to allow the joy of resonance to be your guiding light rather than merely settling for what you *should* be doing. Say "Yes" to that unusual date, take the job that everyone says is beneath you, move to the place that instantly feels like home. Following your heart is how you follow your path. One day when your world is full of love and it feels right, you may look back on this decision and realize it was the most profound moment of your life.

Additional meanings for The Autumn Lovers:

- a connection – romantic, platonic, or spiritual – that feels fated or life altering
- a temptation to take shortcuts
- discovering compatibility through shared values
- deciding between two paths
- online dating, polyamory, or exploring non-traditional relationship structures
- choosing between consumerist desire and deeper values.

VII. The Autumn Chariot

A ghost runs with her companion wolves, which have also crossed beyond the veil. On the surface it appears as though the maiden is being led by the wolves, but notice that her hand rests gently above the creatures. She doesn't need to control them with force or chains. They blend and merge together as they run, becoming not three beings but an integrated whole. Their minds work as one: one direction, one movement, one goal.

Divinatory meaning

The Autumn Chariot is about focus, willpower, and drive. Through the lens of autumn it brings the additional layer of overcoming your fears and past identities. The maiden is a ghost here, having to let go of what it means to be *alive*. She must learn to exist in a new version of herself that will require her to approach this path with sheer determination. There will be obstacles to overcome, and she will need to learn, unlearn, and relearn things as she becomes more familiar with this course. Some days will be harder to control than others, but if she holds her objective as her guiding light she will surely reach her destination.

This card appears to remind you that you can be successful in any goal of your choosing, but that doesn't mean accomplishment will be easy. There will be moments when your challenges will be stronger than you are, when you'll have to remove all distractions and put your energy entirely into your desired outcome. Now is not the time to give in to temptation or allow outside influence to color your vision with doubt.

Additionally, this card reminds you to be adaptable. There will be a lot of moving parts when The Autumn Chariot arrives, meaning you may need to be ready to change course at a moment's notice to avoid danger or unnecessary complications. In this way, this card becomes one of awareness. Taking your eye off the path for even a moment can be enough to completely derail your course.

Additional meanings for The Autumn Chariot:

- moving into a new season, chapter, or territory with deliberate intent
- learning when to grip the reins tightly and when to surrender to the current
- taking control of your professional trajectory rather than waiting for opportunity
- mastering technology as a vehicle of progress
- journeys requiring careful navigation, literal or metaphorical.

VIII. Autumn Strength

The beast the maiden faces takes on something more elemental. Instead of a lion or bear she meets the wind, a symbol of her inner wilderness manifested in her physical world. The wind is untamed, uncontrollable, and often erratic, yet the maiden stays and endures. She doesn't fight what's in front of her: she surrenders to it.

Divinatory meaning

In the fall, Autumn Strength is reframed as the ability to withstand what cannot be controlled. Typically this card features a woman wrestling a lion, which might suggest strength is about gaining power over your wildness. This maiden has no desire to gain power over anything. She doesn't tame her wildness: she befriends it, she embraces it, and she faces it with courage and the knowledge that she can do hard things.

When this card appears it's to remind you that you, too, can stand against adversity, that you can endure the obstacles in front of you. Listen to your instincts and let them work with you rather than fighting for control. Your heart and mind can be partners in finding solutions when you give them equal footing to make decisions.

This card can also represent facing a fear versus trying to avoid it. Humans are much more capable than they allow themselves to believe. Strength isn't found in the moments when the winds are calm and the days are pleasant, it's found among the storms that test your resolve and the situations that force you to be resourceful, calm, and brave.

Additional meanings for Autumn Strength:

- the ability to persist through difficulty, grief, or decline
- resisting the urge to overwork or react aggressively in stressful environments
- providing support to a partner or loved one going through difficulty
- practicing compassion in activism, advocacy, or online spaces
- building resilience during collective crises such as climate change or political unrest.

IX. The Autumn Hermit

A maiden travels through an autumnal cemetery, heading into a large crypt. She holds a lantern in her hands as she knows she is about to face a deep darkness that is beyond anything she's known before, but she isn't afraid. She's taking this pilgrimage as a moment to reflect and reconnect with the innermost part of herself, something she cannot do while among the chatter and distraction of her community. The graveyard represents a connection to spirit, the world beyond the physical. It also represents death, for the maiden is being sent forth upon this journey but the maiden we see here is not the one who will return.

Divinatory meaning

It's quite easy to reduce The Autumn Hermit to an excuse for solitude when, really, this card is about introspection. It appears when your charge is to reconnect with yourself, which doesn't necessarily have to mean being alone for extended periods of time. All that is required is a willingness to rely on your inner knowing, to light your own path rather than waiting for someone else to show you the way.

This card invites you to check in with yourself to see whether you're happy with your journey. Are you still maintaining your values? Do you still believe yourself capable of accomplishing your goals? However, more so than evaluation, this card is about self-value, about knowing yourself and knowing what you have to offer. It's easy to forget how worthy you are when you are distracted by the demands of the world around you.

At its purest form, this card can be a call to engage in a practice of peace such as meditation, hiking, yoga, journaling, or breathwork: a dedicated experience that allows you time to let your mind listen to its own voice. It is within these moments that you will find clarity about your next steps.

Additional meanings for The Autumn Hermit:

+ taking a sabbatical, break, or time away to realign your purpose
+ temporary solitude after a breakup or major change
+ digital minimalism or intentional disconnection from social media
+ remote locations such as mountains, forests, or desert retreats
+ boundary setting around time, availability, or public presence.

X. The Autumn Wheel

A spider has weaved a perfect web. The web is both a trap and a tapestry, suggesting you are both a creator and caught in your own seasons. The spider is in control of this situation, intentionally generating the circumstances necessary to create abundance and success, but something will be caught in her web and luck for that unfortunate being won't be as joyous. However, the spider's fortune will change at some point, and what was the hunter will become the hunted. The only thing you can know for sure is that luck never lasts forever.

Divinatory meaning

The Autumn Wheel is a card of luck and change. Sometimes luck will be good, at other times bad, and often somewhere between the two. Whether you believe in luck or not, change is everyone's lot in life. Whatever you're experiencing today, for better or worse, will come to an end, so take comfort in knowing that your challenge will pass. This card can also indicate a need to take advantage of your good fortune, to be present in your situation rather than looking for danger or additional options.

Typically, this card indicates a fortunate change in your circumstances: if you're experiencing hardship you can rest easy knowing you are nearing the end of that journey. Note, though, that change, no matter how good, can also be challenging. Be mindful not to derail your progress by giving in to the overwhelm and frustration of a moving situation. Regardless of your question, pulling this card indicates a transition is upon you.

Additional meanings for The Autumn Wheel:

- business cycles: booms, busts, or market changes
- learning to flow with a partner's changes instead of clinging to the past
- exploring astrology, lunar cycles, or the wheel of the year
- election cycles, global events, and collective fate intersecting with personal lives
- knowing when to hold steady and when to seize the moment.

XI. Autumn Consequences

A couple stands in silence within their overgrown farm, shock and frustration adorning their faces. They're taking in the unruly weeds and vines that have taken over the once-thriving fruits and vegetables. They've been away for quite some time, choosing to neglect their responsibilities in favor of other choices. With no one there to tend to the plants, the entire farm has taken on a mind of its own. Not only will they have nothing to harvest this fall and winter, but they will also need to work twice as hard to prepare the farm for the following year.

Divinatory meaning

This card is about taking responsibility for your choices and knowing there are consequences for your actions or inactions. When this card appears it can represent rewards for a job well done or making smart decisions. It can mean your efforts are paying off, and all that is coming to you is well deserved. You're getting out what you've put in.

This can be a very positive card indicating a happy outcome. Yes, it can represent something legal as its former name of Justice suggests, such as winning a court battle or having a decision ruled in your favor, but it can also be as mundane as seeing a relationship flourish because you've chosen to offer compassion to your partner or getting a raise at work because you've refused to cut corners. As well, it could indicate paying off a debt because you chose to save rather than splurge.

Another thing this card can represent is a need for accountability. Who are you in this situation: the person who showed integrity and made well-founded decisions, or the person who cut corners, avoided responsibility and expected someone else to pick up the pieces?

This card can feel difficult to receive. You may experience feelings of judgment or harshness, but that isn't the case as this card is unbiased. It doesn't place blame; rather, it invites you to come to your own conclusions about the situation you're facing and how much of a part you've played in it.

Additional meanings for Autumn Consequences:

+ facing the truth, even when it hurts
+ financial audits, taxes, or legal matters coming to light
+ learning to take responsibility rather than blame shifting
+ realizing that the universe is neither punishing nor rewarding
+ consequences of digital footprints: past posts resurfacing.

XII. The Autumn Hanged One

A maiden becomes one with a creature of the night: a bat. Perhaps hanging here among these animals was something she did once in a while but now it has become a part of her being, a normal expression of her everyday life. Transforming into a bat herself represents becoming one with what scares people most: shadow, darkness, the unseen, and the unknown. All around her are signs of pause such as autumn leaves falling, a cup of tea resting gently on a branch, and candlelight illuminating her gaze. The crescent moon reflects reflection and release, and slowing down to gain insight and hidden truths.

Divinatory meaning

The Autumn Hanged One is at home during the darker months of the year such as autumn, the season of surrender, pause, and preparation. When this card arrives it's to encourage you to slow down and take in your surroundings from a new perspective. Change the angle, allowing yourself to consider elements that haven't crossed your mind until now.

Typically, the arrival of this card suggests an urge to rush, force, manipulate, and speed up in an effort to find solutions to your problems, when the opposite is indeed the prescription. You don't need more productivity, resources, answers, or opportunities. What you need now is to flip things upside down and consider what's before you in an entirely different way. In extreme cases, you may need to walk away altogether: not forever but for a time, to disassociate from the situation and return with fresh eyes.

The appearance of The Autumn Hanged One can also indicate a stalled endeavor. This isn't a punishment or a sign to give up, but it could be a summons to reconsider what you believe to be true. Perhaps you're not on the right path or you're going about things in the wrong way. Maybe you need to strip back your ego and reflect on the truth of your situation.

At its very core this card means "not right now." You're not ready to charge ahead with your plans, as more thought, information gathering, or reflection is required at this time.

Additional meanings for The Autumn Hanged One:

- letting go of control and yielding to larger forces
- waiting for the right timing in investments or negotiations
- forced rest such as illness, injury, or burnout
- taking a gap year or time away from formal learning
- trips delayed, rescheduled, or unexpectedly rerouted
- acts of surrender: minimalism, releasing consumerism, or voluntary simplicity.

XIII. Autumn Death

A ghost is making her way between a glowing orb of light: the afterlife. She's disappearing little by little as she ascends, shedding her former incarnation. The road here is littered with mementos of a life lived well, such as the locket of a loved one just to the side. All around her leaves are falling and the landscape is dark. Perhaps this is Samhain night and she is crossing the veil after saying a final goodbye to the life she once knew.

Divinatory meaning

If death could be reduced to one word it would be acceptance. This card appears in the moment when the ending has arrived and there's nothing left to do but move on. There's a finality here, a realization that no amount of pleading or hoping will change your situation. This card indicates something is over but it also serves as permission to grieve, to acknowledge something that mattered to you even if you know it's for the best to let it go.

Death primarily focuses on the end of a chapter, but it also leaves space for a new beginning. In traditional tarot there is a white rose; here, there's a light at the end of the journey. You can't know what comes next but you can know that this isn't truly the end, not for you. It's the end for something – a job, the last days of your child living at home, a dream with no hopes of accomplishment, the end of your college years, or moving away from friends and family – but you will keep going and find a way to thrive in this new leg of your story.

This card comes with a final note of caution: you have to let go. You're in danger of finding yourself in limbo rather than allowing yourself the freedom to explore a different version of yourself. Holding on to what's ending isn't going to stop it from going; it will just stop you from living your life.

Additional meanings for Autumn Death:

- the dismantling of false identity or outdated roles
- breakups, divorce, or the natural end of a connection
- rituals of release: burning, burying, composting the old
- abandoning a course of study that no longer resonates
- rituals of decluttering, downsizing, or simplifying.

XIV. Autumn Temperance

An alchemical witch is working in her apothecary. She's blending liquids, mixing them into perfectly balanced vials and changing their individual structure as each interacts with something new. Perhaps the potions are fine on their own, but she's curious to see what else can be made by bringing separate parts together. This pursuit of balance can be seen all around her. She's creating, yet her space is full of death: dried herbs, skulls, bones, and autumn leaves.

Divinatory meaning

Autumn Temperance is much like autumn: it exists as a liminal energy. The season of autumn brings heat and cold, sun and rain, abundance of last harvests, and the death and decay of the very same plants, but there is no competition during the fall months. Everything exists in balance, a dance of letting go of what was to embrace something new.

Temperance teaches you how to moderate, how to turn away from one extreme or another, blending two separate parts to form a new whole. You may see this manifested in fostering peace between two opposing parties, blending two distinct styles to form something that is uniquely your own, or perhaps taking an old tradition and updating it with new methods. Autumn Temperance is the magic spot, the golden hour of your soul where conditions meet in just the right circumstances to create something showstopping and inspiring. In this way, this card is about integration more than simply balance.

When this card appears it's to encourage you to play the alchemist in your own life, to contemplate compromising paths to solutions rather than choosing a side. You may need to be more receptive to other viewpoints or consider creating a path that is specific to you, your taste, and experience. The best way forward is the option that doesn't require a sacrifice of one thing or the other. In some cases, this card can indicate discovery of the perfect blend of elements, such as a business plan clicking into place or meeting a friend who perfectly complements your energy.

Additional meanings for Autumn Temperance:

- balancing career ambitions with personal well-being
- blending families, cultures, or values into harmony
- tracking seasonal changes in energy and adapting habits accordingly
- integrating shadow and light in spiritual practice
- blending skill sets or perspectives into innovative work.

XV. The Autumn Devil

A maiden sits somberly in her home, the candlelight reflecting her shadow on the wall, but her shadow doesn't take her shape. Instead, it appears as a horned devil looming over her. The maiden gazes at the apple with a bite on the table. You have to wonder what happened here: perhaps she bit the apple in an attempt to better fuel her body but gave up her quest and chose to indulge in something decadent instead. She has allowed this devil to drive her inner yearnings. For the time being, her choices are not her own.

Divinatory meaning

The devil indicates you are more in control than you have allowed yourself to believe. It's easy to assume from the description that the woman is being influenced by a malevolent force when, really, the shadow is just that: her shadow. It's the part of her that seeks destruction and instant gratification, the part that doesn't want her life to change because change represents danger or uncertainty. The maiden sticks to the devil she knows despite the harm it causes.

You will have felt such a devil within you, shadows that encourage you to give in to temptation. However, autumn is the season of shadow work, and while this card may appear destructive on the surface there's a positive meaning too. The Autumn Devil can show you your desires, and can point to liberation from convention and socio-normative behavior. The key isn't to deny yourself indulgence but to be mindful not to become a slave to it.

You are in control; *you* can decide where and how much to invest your efforts. Self-destruction can be both choosing poor habits and choosing to deny expressing yourself to make others comfortable. It can manifest in having an addiction to things such as drugs or alcohol just as easily as being addicted to being skinny or maintaining beauty standards, or it can be the fine line between playing the victim and playing the martyr.

At its root this card reminds you that short-term gains often lead to long-term implications, no matter how well intentioned you may be. Therefore, if you walk away from this card with nothing else, let it be that compromising yourself for a quick but fleeting payoff is ill-advised.

Additional meanings for The Autumn Devil:

- exploitation in systems that thrive on disempowerment
- staying in jobs for security while feeling trapped
- obsession, jealousy, or unhealthy attachment
- confronting impulses, fantasies, or obsessions
- being drawn to relationships marked by secrecy, taboo, or power imbalance.

XVI. The Autumn Tower

A home is ablaze against a night sky. What was once a source of protection and comfort is now the scene of chaos and destruction, an identity changed in an instant. Signs of a life lived are scattered among the yard, such as a chair in the garden and boots left behind in the rush to find safety. It can't be known what will come next for the people who dwelled here, only that the life they once knew is no longer the life they'll have going forward.

Divinatory meaning

There are some events that are so complete, so thorough, they've changed your entire trajectory, and there are occurrences that are so sudden and violent in their destruction that nothing can put them right. The Autumn Tower represents such circumstances: the situations you didn't see coming yet will have the biggest impact on your life moving forward. When something devastating happens – a home flooded, a partner seeking a divorce, a diagnosis, or a layoff from a job when you've just bought a house – all you're left with is a clean slate to start over.

When this card appears it's to remind you what can happen when you over-identify with something. Sometimes you'll give so much value to things that don't really matter at all, at least not in the grand scheme of things. Perhaps your attachment to something has prevented you from living the life you desire in your dreams, or maybe you've stayed right where you are out of fear of what might happen if you dared to do something different. It may not feel like it at this moment but The Autumn Tower's destruction is a path to liberation, a chance for you to make an intentional decision about what your life can look like.

This card can also be something you've decided for yourself. You may wish to burn down a bridge just for the sake of making something final. It can be symbolic, representing a breakthrough or dramatic shift in perspective rather than a physical hardship. However The Autumn Tower manifests itself, all that will be left to do after the dust settles is to move on and chart a new course from here.

Additional meanings for The Autumn Tower:

- exposed scandals or corruption
- discovering betrayal or infidelity
- health crises or wake-up calls that demand immediate attention
- intense lessons learned through failure or disruption
- secrets spilling out at the dinner table
- a research discovery that invalidates years of work.

XVII. The Autumn Star

A maiden stands before a still pool, her presence quiet yet radiant beneath the autumn sky. She wears a cloak of plum lined with gold, echoing the dying leaves around her. In her hands she holds a vessel that pours glowing water – starlight itself – into the dark pool, weaving heaven and earth into one. The water ripples with tiny stars, as though the night sky has descended into the world below.

Around the maiden a circle of candles stand upright and flickering. Each flame is an offering, a wish, a grief, a prayer, illuminating the shadows of the forest. Moths hover nearby, drawn to the glow and reminding you of your soul's instinctive longing for light. Above her the moon and stars shine in witness, their eternal presence promising renewal even in the deepening dark.

Divinatory meaning

The Autumn Star represents a moment of peace after the truly devastating events of The Autumn Tower. This is perhaps the first chance in a long time to simply relax and feel safe, supported, or comfortable. This card can also represent a rebirth, a time when you can finally contemplate what comes next without worrying about what you've lost. It's a time to dream again, to imagine what's possible now that the dust has finally settled.

When this card appears it's a reminder that the worst is behind you. That isn't to say you won't ever have challenges, but it does mean the ground won't shift beneath your feet like it has in the past. Therefore, this card can also represent healing, a return to feeling like yourself or just restoring your sense of equilibrium.

Receiving this card may serve as encouragement to start a healing journey, one that helps you to further process and release your grief, or it may simply be a reminder that hope is always a worthy goal. Things may not be perfect but you can see the light at the end of the tunnel, and even just that bit of positivity can make a world of difference.

Additional meanings for The Autumn Star:

- reconnecting with your higher self or spirit guides
- rebuilding communities or identities after a crisis
- a renewed vision for your career path or creative projects
- using creativity or spirituality as medicine in uncertain times
- forgiveness and renewal in strained bonds.

XVIII. Waning Moon

A maiden has drifted to a small pond, drawn in by the allure of a big, bright crescent moon. She's been wandering for a long time, trying to get a sense of where she is, and she realizes she's lost because the moon has descended from the sky and is no longer lighting her way. She dips her toes into the water, convinced this moon bath isn't real: all this does is further distort the image in front of her. Is she dreaming? Is she really here? She can feel the truth nearby, yet it continues to elude her.

Divinatory meaning

In autumn The Moon is renamed Waning Moon to represent darkness, intuition, and inner reflection. Just like a waning moon there is a need to turn inward, trusting in your own guidance rather than trying to make sense of what's in front of you. Your situation is an illusion, a half-truth or shadow masquerading as something more sinister than reality.

This card doesn't mean anything good or bad; it simply means something is distorted. Old fears may be resurfacing, convincing you there's danger when there is not, or perhaps the opposite is true and you are so enamored by the illusion that you cannot see red flags that have gone beyond your notice. Waning Moon has appeared not to convince you there is anything right or wrong with your circumstances, but to invite you to dive deeper, look beyond what you can see, and check in with the part of you that can separate truth from fiction.

This card will often appear when there's a sense of disorientation. Perhaps each subtle shift in behavior has spooked you so much that you're ready to give up altogether. If that is the case, take a moment to pause and gather yourself. Deep down you know what to do, and you just need to remember to check in with yourself.

Additional meanings for Waning Moon:

- navigating places or cultures where you don't fully understand the language
- exploring psychology, myth, dream studies, or occult subjects
- rituals tied to the waning moon: release, cleansing, banishing
- psychosomatic symptoms: your body mirroring subconscious fears
- being caught in projection: seeing someone as you wish them to be, not as they are.

XIX. Sunset

The image is simple, as it represents pure joy. A maiden is dancing with wild abandon among a field of wildflowers at a golden hour. She's free and full of light and a zest for life. She's been through a lot in somewhat recent times, but she's finally reconnected with her seat of energy and radiance.

Divinatory meaning

In autumn Sunset (also known as The Sun) takes on a different kind of happiness. This is earned joy, the kind that can only be found by facing the hardest moments of your life and still finding a way to thrive. Through the lens of autumn this card represents fighting for your right to be okay, to embrace life despite the times you've wondered whether or not the universe truly had your back. The maiden is not a babe like you would see in traditional tarot. She isn't naive or innocent: she's weathered and tested, making this return to happiness all the more sweet.

The appearance of this card is an immediate call to seek positivity and radiance in your life, to invest time and effort into the things that light you up. It can also mean times are really good or will be very soon. There's no need to question the sudden shift in fortunes, especially not with Sunset as you have earned the right to be happy.

This card can also represent true alignment, confidence, and the ability to bet on yourself without fear of judgment or validation. You truly are in your element when this card appears, and all people or situations tied to this card have a warm light upon them as well.

Additional meanings for Sunset:

- energy, health, and enthusiasm returning
- clarity in career direction or financial choices
- public recognition: social media visibility, platforms growing
- successful unions, marriages, or reunions
- child-like playfulness or renewal in intimacy.

XX. Reckoning

Numerous mirrors sit within a room, each reflecting a different version of the same maiden. Some are past versions of her, while others are unlived aspects and dreams. In the center stands the real maiden gazing into the only mirror that shows her truth as she knows it. She's facing herself, reclaiming all parts of who she was and who she is and, in so doing, becoming whole.

Divinatory meaning

Unlike the traditional Judgment card, Reckoning isn't about being judged by a higher, holier power but is about facing *yourself*: fully, honestly, and without fear. This is the moment when you take the masks off and the stories you've told yourself collapse, when every part of your being looks you directly in the eye and asks: "Who do you want to be?"

When you look at this card from that angle you can see there is no outside savior waiting to show you your path. You are the witness to your story and the judge of how you've lived your life. When you gaze at your own reflection what do you see: a life lived well, or one that needs a change?

When this card appears it stands as a moment to reflect on how far you've come for better or worse, to evaluate your accomplishments and then decide what comes next. In its most positive form this card is about evolution and acknowledging that you're ready for the next phase of your journey. Reflection then becomes a moment to praise past versions of yourself for getting you here, and also a chance to say goodbye before shedding your current identity once again.

This card can also represent a moment of clinging to outdated stories of yourself. In that case it has appeared to urge you to let go of what is already gone. You cannot ascend to a new level while clinging on to an old version. In either case, this card represents renewal. This is the moment before a new season begins, and its presence is inviting you to prepare by releasing what is no longer serving your story.

Additional meanings for Reckoning:

- learning from past failures with a new perspective
- recognizing lifestyle consequences and making corrections
- returning to an old love or relationship dynamic for closure or renewal
- rebranding, relaunching, or resurrecting a business idea
- hearing a spiritual call to a new path, practice, or role.

XXI. Descending to Winter

A new season is now upon the maiden. She sits by her window gazing out at the first snow of the year. The leaves are still vibrant with shades of amber, gold, and brown, but the landscape is covered with a thin blanket of white. She loves autumn, but she knows seasons will come and go. For now she's ready to welcome winter and all of the lessons that will surely come with it.

Divinatory meaning

Autumn is coming to a close when Descending to Winter appears. You'll likely know this card as The World, a card of completion, success and, ultimately, new beginnings. This is the moment when one season in your life ends and it drops you right back at The Fool to start the journey all over again, only this time progressing through winter.

This card appears at the end of a chapter, but it invites you to be mindful to stop here for a moment. Allow yourself to be in this liminal space between what was and what will be. You have been successful; you have overcome obstacles, risen to many occasions, and confronted hard truths. Allow yourself now this opportunity to let it all sink in.

It's not uncommon to draw this card after monumental life events such as a marriage, birth, graduation, or promotion, or a significant move such as building your dream home or retirement. In moments like these it's important to simply be where you are, to contemplate what it means to have made it, and to have reached the goal and consider for a brief time how this will impact your life going forward.

There will be plenty of time for new adventures – you still have plenty of story to write – but for now release the sense of urgency to get somewhere. Drawing this card means you've already arrived.

Additional meanings for Descending to Winter:

- celebrating anniversaries, commitments, or milestones
- the closing of cultural eras, movements, or trends
- completing long-term study, an apprenticeship, or a project
- acceptance of ageing, cycles, or bodily change
- feeling complete and whole within yourself, no longer needing external validation.

Minor arcana

The minor arcana makes up the vast majority of the tarot, mostly because they represent the everyday goings on in life. These are the emotions, sensations, and perspectives that show up unexpectedly in ordinary situations such as driving to work, date night, standing in line for a coffee, or in the middle of that really important meeting. So much emphasis is given to the major arcana when it's the minor arcana that truly shows you how to move from one state of being to the next. Individually, each minor arcana card may seem insignificant, but when combined they tell a narrative of where you've been, where you are and, ultimately, where you're going.

There are four suits within the minor arcana: wands, cups, swords, and pentacles. The names have changed only slightly in *Autumn Tarot*, but the symbolism used to convey them is completely different from what you might be familiar with. Wands are represented by broomsticks, cups by jack-o'-lanterns, swords by branches, and pentacles by mirrors. Navigate to the beginning of each section to find out more about why we've chosen these symbols and how they represent autumn.

Each suit also has four court cards. Many believe the court cards represent people, which is true in some cases, but I have always found them to be archetypes to aspire to, not unlike the major arcana. In *Autumn Tarot* I have renamed them to better illustrate the evolutionary quality of each suit while also eliminating a specific gender narrative.

In this tarot pages are known as initiates. This will be the same in all four of the *Seasons of the Witch* tarots as a page's role is to be at the beginning and to learn how to receive. Knights are renamed seekers, as a knight's role is to pursue: they have a longing to accomplish something and are brave in their efforts to reach this goal. Queens are named shepherds here. Queens are often seen as having supporting yet powerful roles, nourishing, guiding, and offering a gentle hand, just like a shepherd carrying for his flock. Kings are renamed keepers. Kings protect, preserve, and serve as the mastery of the suite or, in this case, they serve as the keepers of each suit's energy, the holder of its legacy.

Autumn Wands

For the suit of Wands Tijana and I have decided to use broomsticks in place of traditional wands. However, the names have stayed the same to make it easier to identify each card's energy. Wands traditionally symbolize passion, energy, and action, and brooms enhance this by adding a layer of magic, cleansing, and directed intent. Brooms are also inherently transitional: they sweep away the old to make room for the new, perfectly capturing the energy of change represented by the autumn season. Also like wands, brooms represent progress. In the suit of Wands the transformation from idea, with the Ace of Autumn Wands, to the weight of responsibility success often brings, represented by the Ten of Autumn Wands, can be seen.

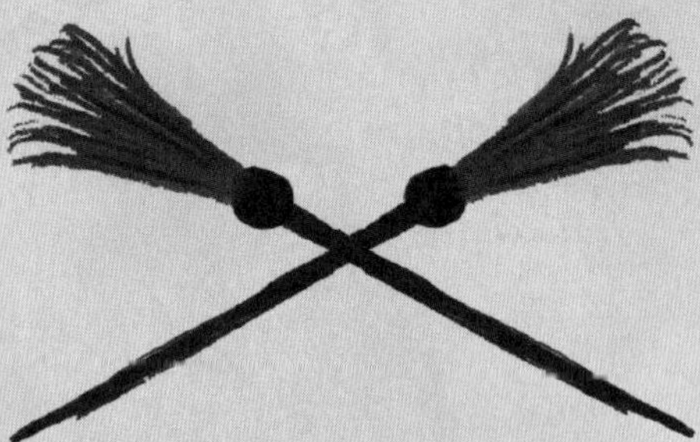

Ace of Autumn Wands

The Ace of Autumn Wands marks a moment of inspiration, a download of new ideas, but in autumn the traditional Ace of Wands takes on a different layer of creative spark. In summer or spring this burst of ideas might seem bold, sudden, and energetic, while in autumn the Ace of Wands is about resonance. It represents the joy and inspiration that can be had when tapping into the resources and ideas you already have rather than struggling to create something entirely new.

New beginnings don't have to mean starting completely from scratch. Sometimes the most profound sparks of brilliance occur when you stop trying to force and, instead, learn to move with the season you're in. They occur when you stop trying to manufacture an outcome and simply allow yourself the space to let everything click into place.

When this card appears it invites you to find different ways to use the time, resources, and paths you already have. Perhaps you should try doing something old in a new way or an old idea is given fresh energy. As with all aces, the window of opportunity is slim and doesn't leave much room for doubt. Don't hesitate to act upon an idea when it comes: tap into this burst of fresh energy and make the most of it.

Additional meanings for the Ace of Autumn Wands:

- buying tickets, booking a trip, or saying "Yes" before thinking things through
- physically sweeping, painting, or rearranging a room to welcome new energy
- the spark of a new romance or rekindled passion in an existing one
- burnout if the spark isn't channeled wisely
- rediscovering the simple joy of experimentation, trying something new, or approaching something with whimsy and wonder.

Two of Autumn Wands

A maiden sits in a tree, contemplating what her plans will be and where she'll go. She has her broom next to her, but she's making a new broom as she watches the night sky go by with the idea that this new broom will take her even further than the last.

The Two of Autumn Wands represents the moment immediately after a spark of inspiration, the space where a new idea begins to take shape. Plans begin to form and possibilities make your idea all the more exciting. However, this is also the moment to evaluate what should come with you on this new journey and what needs to be rebuilt or replaced, for what got you here may not carry you forward.

In this way the Two of Autumn Wands can also represent the edge of your comfort zone. You can continue to choose what is familiar but you must do so knowing you will be limited in your results, or you can expand your horizons by doing what is necessary to meet new challenges.

Additional meanings for the Two of Autumn Wands:

- early stages of launching a project: drafting a proposal, making plans, or strategizing growth
- having conversations about the future such as long-term plans, living together, marriage, or children
- preparing physically for a challenge
- choosing between saving safely or taking calculated financial risks for greater growth
- the bittersweet longing to explore beyond your current dynamic.

Three of Autumn Wands

The Ace of Autumn Wands represents inspiration and the Two of Autumn Wands represents planning. Now the Three of Autumn Wands represents growth, the natural progression of creative energy. You've done all of the planning and preparation you can do and there's nothing left to be done but to act. This card invites your courage to rise to the occasion. It's time to test the resources you've gathered to see if they measure up to this new horizon. That is what growth is: a decision to move beyond your comfort zone.

This card appearing in your spread is a sign that the moment you've been preparing for has arrived. It's time to submit your manuscript, ask for a promotion, put up that first post online, or finally take the jump to become a professional tarot reader.

This card can also signal that your past efforts are beginning to bear fruit. Growth is happening steadily, even if it doesn't look grand or dramatic. Like autumn itself expansion can be subtle yet undeniable, a slow coloring of leaves that signals inevitable change. Keep putting in the effort and challenging yourself, and trust that new opportunities are aligning ready for you to seize when they arrive.

Additional meanings for the Three of Autumn Wands:

- testing a business idea by officially launching your first product or service
- choosing to expand your emotional comfort zone by being more vulnerable or expressive
- following through on a health change you've been planning: actually starting the diet, routine, or therapy
- seeing early returns on previous investments, with more growth ahead
- traveling for opportunity: relocation, study abroad, or business expansion.

Four of Autumn Wands

The Four of Autumn Wands is a card of celebration and an acknowledgment of milestones. It's so easy to look at the traditional card and think of marriage as that is what the imagery has conditioned us to see, but this card goes far beyond just a romantic union. It can represent a birth, graduation, anniversary, career-defining promotion, holiday, or even a significant shift in your personal journey.

The additional layer of autumn brings the perspective of gratitude, especially when milestones are shared among others. When this card appears it's to encourage you to pause and enjoy the fruits of your labor rather than rushing off to the next goal or task, to look around with pride and revel in all of the actions that have led you to this moment.

Outside of achievement, this card can simply be your invitation to enjoy life: there needn't be a success to celebrate. Gather and experience joy because it's Tuesday or because you've survived some challenging times. Be in good company because you all love Samhain and wish to commune with others who share your values, or just because you know some really great people who are always up for a good time.

Additionally, autumn reminds you that celebration itself is an act of courage. To feast in a season when you have no reason to is to say: *we have enough, we are enough, and what we share is sacred.*

Additional meanings for the Four of Autumn Wands:

- achieving stability after a period of struggle
- reaching a health milestone: a weight goal, healing progress, or recovery marker
- a happy homecoming or family celebration
- company anniversary, grand opening, or successful project completion
- engagements, weddings, anniversaries, or moving in together.

Five of Autumn Wands

Five witches clash with their brooms, their energy colliding in a swirl of motion and intense emotion. No one is truly winning, yet no one is willing to let go. This is the nature of the Five of Autumn Wands: a contest of wills where pride and passion can eclipse purpose and understanding.

This is a card of conflict, competition, and scattered energy. Your charge is a worthy cause, so much so that others have had the same spark of inspiration and now everyone is fighting for their right to be heard. There's an assumption that you're missing out on something if you don't fight when, perhaps, you didn't listen long enough to understand what's actually happening.

This card appears to invite you to take a step back, to disengage from the fight and fully look at the situation before projecting your thoughts and ideas. Receiving this card is often a sign that everyone involved wants the same things but is also too busy fighting to recognize you're on the same team.

Additional meanings for the Five of Autumn Wands:

- office politics, clashing visions, or too many voices in the room
- feeling caught up in comparison, measuring your path against others
- a period of turbulence, conflict, or friction that must be navigated before progress can occur
- disrupted travel plans due to clashing schedules, logistical chaos, or competing priorities
- household tension over chores, responsibilities, or conflicting personalities
- choosing to win rather than listening or collaborating.

Six of Autumn Wands

A witch with broom in hand stands tall and regal under a big, bright, full moon for all the world to see. She can't hide her achievements anymore – her reputation precedes her now – and she doesn't want to. She's proud of who she is and what she's accomplished, so she happily allows those around her to sing her praises.

Receiving this card is a sign of recognition. You are being watched closely because you've done something remarkable or, at the very least, worthy of a second glance, and you've earned this. Do not mistake this praise as a source of good luck: you've put in the work and made the tough choices, and now you'll reap the rewards. However, this card invites you to step even further into the spotlight, to celebrate your success and allow yourself to feel the warmth of being acknowledged. It also reminds you that what you do with your visibility matters more than the applause itself.

There is a shadow here, of course. Allowing yourself to be seen can be an act of courage in itself for it requires a deep level of vulnerability. To be the center of attention invites admiration but also criticism and even envy. The witch is adored now, but will that last? She must avoid the temptation of complacency and continue the efforts that won her this recognition.

Additional meanings for the Six of Autumn Wands:

- feeling seen and appreciated by your partner
- being asked to lead, teach, or offer your practice to others
- public acknowledgment within weeks
- recognition within the family for your role or contribution
- external validation becoming more important than private truth.

Seven of Autumn Wands

In the old ways a broom would be hung over the door of a home to guard against unwanted spirits and ill will. The Seven of Autumn Wands carries this same protective energy, appearing when you feel the need to defend your boundaries and protect the space you've worked so hard to create.

This is not a card of aggression, but one of resolve. You feel as though you're being tested with gossip, envy, or small but persistent challenges: obstacles that seem insignificant on their own, but when compounded they become a weight that is much too heavy to bear. The Seven of Autumn Wands appears to tell you to be vigilant, to understand that some unwelcome guests may be knocking on your door. You do not have to invite them in: not every opinion deserves your ear or consideration.

The additional layer of autumn reminds you that protection is sacred work that must be tended to. Just as leaves fall to shield roots over winter and fires protect homes from the cold, your job now is to safeguard your progress, peace, and accomplishments. Reaching a goal isn't the final destination; how you keep it is what matters.

Additional meanings for the Seven of Autumn Wands:

- standing firm in your ideas or methods despite criticism
- protecting your privacy or personal space when others overstep
- resisting the urge to explain or justify your path to others
- a season of tests or pushback
- spending too much energy fighting small battles instead of focusing on the big picture.

Eight of Autumn Wands

The Eight of Autumn Wands is a card of momentum, appearing when the pace of life speeds up and everything begins to move all at once. It's not unlike the energy of autumn: one moment the branches are heavy with green leaves, and the next leaves are swirling around on the wind in shades of brown, amber, and gold.

This card arrives when events accelerate, messages arrive, or opportunities present themselves all at once. The whirlwind can feel exhilarating, like finally catching a current that carries you forward after a long struggle, but it can also feel disorienting if you're not grounded in your purpose or if you don't have a sense of where you wish to go from here.

When the Eight of Autumn Wands appears, expect progress, rapid change, or a sense that things are quickly falling into place. Trust the pace, but stay focused on where you want this current to take you. The winds will carry you, but not if you resist the momentum when it comes.

Additional meanings for the Eight of Autumn Wands:

- sudden job offers, interviews, or promotions arriving all at once
- a project moving ahead faster than expected
- money coming in suddenly: bonuses, invoices paid, unexpected financial support
- passionate encounters, whirlwind romances, or quick reconciliations
- a sudden breakthrough
- becoming overwhelmed by too much energy or input at once.

Nine of Autumn Wands

The Nine of Autumn Wands whispers a message to you: *hold fast. You are on the cusp of completion. The next season will bring a release, but first you must endure this final passage.*

This card represents endurance. It appears when you're tired, worn out, and ready to quit; however, it also means you're closer to completion than you realize. The additional layer of autumn reframes this card as the exhaustion of thresholds: that heavy, liminal space where endings and beginnings overlap. You're neither here nor there, and holding both spaces is challenging your strength.

Receiving this card is an acknowledgment of your fatigue, but it also affirms your resilience. You have weathered storms, defended your ground, and pushed through obstacles and now the threshold is before you: you're almost there. Do not mistake tiredness for failure, and do not mistake frustration as a sign to quit. Perseverance at this point when you most want to give up is what will carry you across the finish line.

Additional meanings for the Nine of Autumn Wands:

- the need for stamina during the final stretch before success
- enduring the last phase of debt repayment or financial restructuring
- enduring a dark night of the soul as a necessary part of transition
- sticking to a health plan even when progress feels slow
- exhaustion during travel: long journeys, delays, or challenges along the way.

Ten of Autumn Wands

This card appears when passion turns into obligation and inspiration is buried beneath exhaustion. It represents the times you have worked yourself to the bone, doing for everyone else while ignoring the warning signs that you cannot go on like this.

This is burnout, depletion, being over-needed, and the cost of carrying too much. There's nothing wrong with acts of service and carrying responsibility, but when they strip you of joy and vitality they no longer serve you or those you love. This card reminds you that you cannot continue without rest, regardless of how dedicated or committed you are.

When the Ten of Autumn Wands appears it is both a warning and an invitation. It warns that you may be carrying more than is sustainable, stretching yourself far too thin in the name of proving worth, keeping up with demands, or honoring agreements. It invites you to lay some of that burden down and ask for help or simply learn to say "No!" Rest is not failure or an indication of your value; it's part of the journey and it's definitely within your right to demand it.

Additional meanings for the Ten of Autumn Wands:

- taking on too many projects or responsibilities at once
- managing multiple expenses, bills, or financial obligations
- a spiritual practice that feels like obligation rather than devotion
- over-exertion in fitness routines without rest or recovery
- resentment or collapse when unspoken burdens become too heavy
- mistaking busyness for productivity.

Initiate of Autumn Wands

Someone who is expressing Initiate of Autumn Wands energy is eager to prove themselves. They have plenty of ideas and all of the energy to get things started, but they lack experience and staying power. Novelty is what drives them, not accomplishment. They love the feel of discovery, which often manifests as them taking on a task that is greater than their skill. This can get them into trouble, but it can also awaken many talents within them. The role of the Initiate of Autumn Wands is to teach you to temper enthusiasm with patience and mindfulness.

This card appears when passion and curiosity are upon you. It's a sign to follow this spark to experiment, explore, or begin something new even when you don't know where it will lead you. Step into the role of apprentice and learn to tend to the flames flickering within you, but do so with care. Action is encouraged here, but calculated risks more so than recklessness. This card invites you to learn to sustain your excitement rather than burning through it all at once.

This card so easily drifts into shadow when your flame may be wasted if it is scattered across too many half-finished projects, or dangerous if it's pursued without thought of the consequences. Passion alone isn't enough: you must learn to find focus. Without grounding the initiate burns far too bright and fast, and will quickly fizzle out.

Additional meanings for the Initiate of Autumn Wands:

+ taking on more than you can manage due to excitement
+ a young family member bringing energy, curiosity, or playful chaos into the home
+ spending money impulsively on hobbies or passions
+ flirtation, playful dating, or the spark of attraction.

Seeker of Autumn Wands

A witch throws herself into the air without waiting for permission. She rides fast and wild, sometimes backward or sideways, more concerned with the thrill of flight than with where she'll land. This card captures that restless drive to leap before you've mapped the course, to feel the wind in your hair and trust that motion itself will teach you what the mind cannot.

The Seeker of Autumn Wands is even more of a risk taker than the Initiate of Autumn Wands. The initiate took risks because of a lack of experience, whereas the seeker knows full well what they're doing. They may thrive on reckless behavior and daredevil stunts and they love to push the boundaries, seeing just how far they can take something. To their credit, they often pull it off. This Seeker of Autumn Wands is the evolutionary energy that drives you to expand your horizons by dismantling your comfort zone. The seeker is always looking for ways to do and be more and to experience more.

As an evolutionary energy, the seeker urges you to follow your passion with courage. Adventure calls, and the only way forward is through action. You may not feel fully ready, but readiness is rarely the point: it is the act of daring that ignites the fire. The Seeker of Autumn Wands teaches that progress is found in motion, not in having perfect plans.

This card also invites you to temper this boldness with caution, as some risks aren't worth the bruises. The shadow of this card warns of the costs of impulsivity, scattered efforts, and burning yourself out by chasing thrill after thrill. The challenge is not to extinguish your courage, but to direct it in a meaningful way.

Additional meanings for the Seeker of Autumn Wands:

- quitting a job suddenly to pursue something more exciting
- diving head-first into love without worrying about the outcome
- using money to fuel adventure or freedom rather than stability
- restlessness in the home
- rapid change or opportunities that require quick decisions

Shepherd of Autumn Wands

The Shepherd of Autumn Wands is the full embodiment of the suit of Wands. She is passionate, a visionary and, above all, she is confident. That burst of arrogance with the Seeker of Autumn Wands has paid off: the shepherd knows her boundaries, having tested them many times over. She knows how far she can push herself as well as how far she can push others before their breaking point, a skill she uses to her advantage though many will happily do her bidding. She's as charming and radiant as she is sure of herself.

As an evolutionary energy, the Shepherd of Autumn Wands protects your right to shine. Stop shrinking yourself to fit smaller spaces or dimming your light to make others comfortable. The shepherd teaches that confidence is not arrogance but your truth fully embraced, the natural fire that happens when you stand fully in who you are. She urges you to express your passions boldly, share your gifts openly, and step into the room as though you belong there, because if you're in that room then it means you do.

In shadow the shepherd warns against letting brilliance slip into performance. The glow will not last if your fire burns only for external validation. The danger lies in mistaking applause for authenticity. True confidence is not loud or theatrical, but is grounded and rooted in self-acceptance.

Additional meanings for the Shepherd of Autumn Wands:

- learning how to lead with confidence and charisma
- a relationship flourishing when both people express their full selves
- a season of confidence and visibility
- feeling magnetic: easily drawing admiration or attention
- inspiring others by example rather than instruction.

Keeper of Autumn Wands

The Keeper of Autumn Wands is an opposing flame against a night sky. He is bold, confident, and inspiring and has no problem leading others; in fact, he loves being in that position as it allows him the chance to shape those who follow him, helping them reach their greatness just as he has done.

As an evolutionary energy this card appears to call you to leadership. You may not have asked for it, but you are meant for it. You have the vision and courage to be a light in the darkness for others, just as the Keeper of Autumn Wands is doing for you now. The keeper is not the inexperienced youthfulness of the initiate or the reckless energy of the seeker. The keeper embodies the maturity of passion, directing his energy toward something that will last long after he's gone.

The keeper's invitation is clear: act boldly, but with awareness of your impact. Your fire has grown too large to exist only for yourself, and what you create now has the power to inspire others or consume them in manipulative ways. In shadow this card warns against arrogance, domination, or using influence carelessly. A torch raised high can light a path, but it can also scorch if wielded without integrity.

Additional meanings for the Keeper of Autumn Wands:

- guiding others through mentorship or example
- using resources to create stability and growth for the future
- taking command of your well-being with disciplined, long-term choices
- sharing knowledge generously
- burdening yourself with responsibility or being too controlling.

Autumn Cups

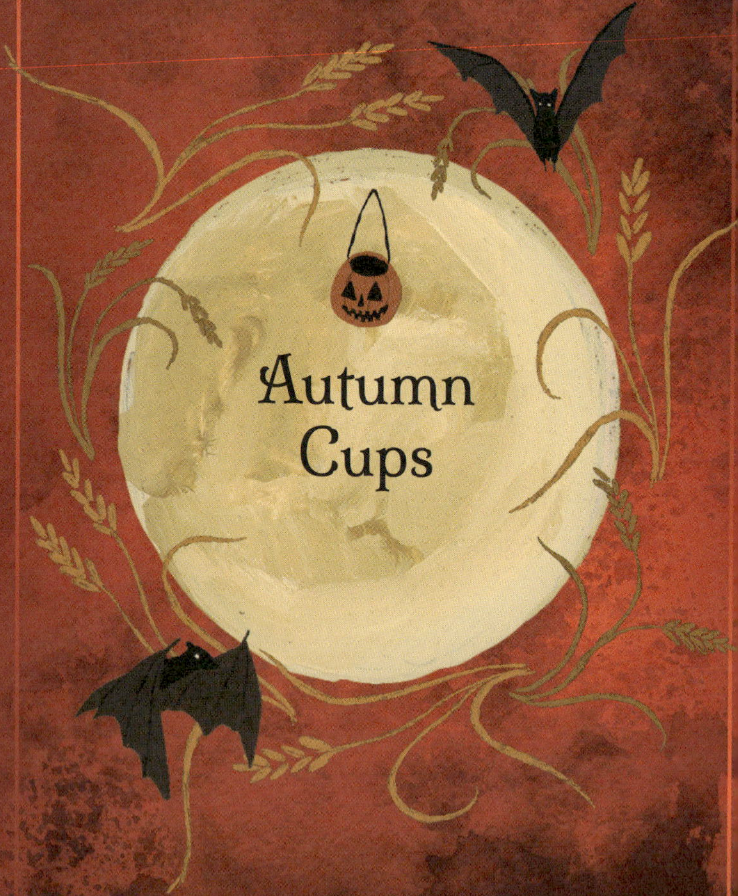

Traditional cups are replaced by jack-o'-lanterns in autumn, an inspired idea of Tijana's that brings a deep level of warmth and whimsy to the most heartfelt of the suits. Traditionally, Cups represent the heart, emotions, and intuition. Jack-o'-lanterns evoke the themes of light in the darkness, emotional warmth, and celebration amid mystery. They symbolize the balance of light and shadow and the joy of connection during transitional times. Jack-o'-lanterns also carry a festive energy, tying into your soul's inner light, which mirrors the depth of emotional introspection the suit of Cups often conveys.

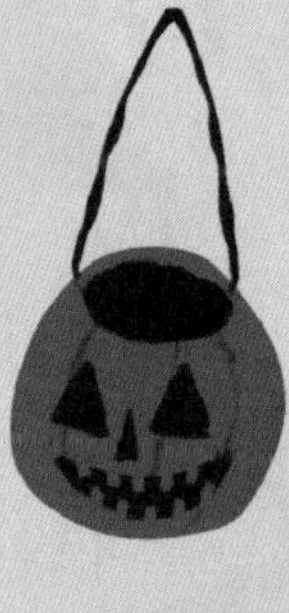

Ace of Autumn Cups

Love through the lens of autumn is different: it's an intentional act, one deliberately claimed after past wounds have healed. This love is earned and fought for, and arrives with the knowledge that love can also wither and die if not tended to properly. It's free of the naiveté of youthful infatuation or the all-consuming attraction of passionate lust. This love is grounded in the desire to be raw and vulnerable despite knowing the sting of loss.

The Ace of Autumn Cups appears as the first spark of recovery from heartbreak as an invitation to try again after being hollowed out of what didn't serve. You've done the work, learned the lessons, and healed your pain, and now you're emotionally ready to claim a connection that matches your strength. The presence of this card also means an opportunity is ripe for the taking; however, this is only a tiny ember, and you're still responsible for fanning the flames. You may be ready to open your heart, but that doesn't mean you're ready to let someone or something in. This chance at connection could pass you by if you linger in apprehension for too long.

Additional meanings for the Ace of Autumn Cups:

+ rebalancing of hormones or cycles after emotional stress
+ reconnecting with an estranged friend or family member
+ starting a new business after a previous one failed
+ recovery from depression or emotional numbness
+ saying "Yes" to a first date or chance at friendship.

Two of Autumn Cups

The Two of Autumn Cups introduces a pair of social outcasts. They appear to be strange and dark and certainly do not fit into society's idea of an inspirational love, yet they've found a resonance in each other despite mourning what it feels like to be labeled *other*. Vulnerability can be the beginning of intimacy, and their ability to hold space for one another has led to a love that is free from judgment and expectation.

It's so easy to lose yourself in the desire to find a soul mate in this card, and it does represent that in many ways. There's a soul deep connection here, but it isn't written in romantic fantasy.

This card speaks to the hardships of real life and how it so rarely matches your imagination.

The Two of Autumn Cups represents an intentional union born not out of explosive chemistry, but from purpose and care. It's a reminder that love needn't be loud or intense to be real, and that two people offering mutual support and steady partnership in the face of obstacles is often much more valuable than the feeling of love at first sight or the desire for love to look good on paper.

That isn't to say chemistry isn't important or a legitimate pathway to connection. However, it isn't the only sign of a promising relationship: be it intimate love, a partnership, friend, or even animal companion. Love is most lasting when built on respect, commitment, and shared effort.

Additional meanings for the Two of Autumn Cups:

- two trauma survivors building something meaningful
- queer love that doesn't mirror heteronormative ideals
- the quiet steadiness of a caregiver/patient bond
- being seen for the first time without needing to perform or assimilate
- meeting someone later than expected or after the fall of something else
- building a relationship that doesn't look ideal but feels deeply right.

Three of Autumn Cups

The Three of Autumn Cups represents a safe space where you're free to celebrate with people who accept you for who you are. Happiness is fleeting at the best of times but is made all the more special when others can share in your joy without competition or malice. It appears when an attachment to something or someone can lead to communal magic, when shared evenings turn into early mornings, or there is elation at being lifted up and claimed by community.

Happiness is a found family, a connection with people who aren't bound by obligation: they choose to stay. You may witness this most readily in the glow of marriage, birth, or the adoption of a child, colleagues toasting to a hard-won success, or a gathering of witches casting a spell, but it could just as easily go much deeper than that. This card can foretell the presence of relationships that are destined to root beyond the surface, the kinds of connections that weather decay, rot, and winter storms and then bloom again as though nothing ever happened. It's a bond forged in the shared experience of being totally different yet exactly the same.

Additional meanings for the Three of Autumn Cups:

+ the necessity of celebrating something, even if it's small
+ feeling unfiltered joy because someone else is feeling it too
+ entering a season where you'll feel emotionally carried by others
+ finding or about to find people who feel like *your* people
+ rebuilding trust in others after isolation.

Four of Autumn Cups

The root of this card is protective withdrawal. It may be a defense against emotional overwhelm, the inability to grab hold of an opportunity, or a flat-out refusal of what's being offered. You can't know for sure as the only thing you're witnessing is a moment of hesitation. What you do know is that a lifeline is available should you want it. There is a sense of abundance for the figure has many jack-o'-lanterns to choose from, with one directly in his line of sight.

This card thus represents the contemplation of what comes next. Perhaps what you have is enough; maybe your harvest is plenty and to pick more would only end up in rot and waste when this offering can go to someone else. A missed opportunity isn't necessarily a mistake if it's refused with intention and careful consideration. Sometimes a withdrawal from the allure of novelty is required to avoid surface-level attachments, while at other times things simply don't feel aligned and you're content to wait for something better.

In a darker expression this card represents emotional numbness. In this case you're unable to receive: invitations are offered but you've normalized a lack of connection or stopped believing in the value of support. The trouble with this is that the world keeps moving even when you're standing still, and if you aren't careful the olive branches will stop being offered and withdrawal will turn into isolation.

Additional meanings for the Four of Autumn Cups:

- symptoms of mild depression or social withdrawal
- ignoring a compliment, opportunity, or gesture of kindness because you don't feel as though you're worthy
- choosing depth over novelty
- intentionally slowing down to listen inward
- telling yourself you're fine when you're actually numb.

Five of Autumn Cups

Autumn is the season of mourning, the time of the year when you honor what you've lost. This card will always represent a moment of grief, regardless if it appears in summer, spring, fall, or winter. The difference with the Five of Autumn Cups is that this sorrow is welcome.

You're not being asked to heal your grief when this card arrives, but to honor it. You mourn because what's lost is missed, and you cry because you ache for something that mattered. To move beyond this anguish, to simply act as though it doesn't exist without the proper time to hold space for it, would diminish the weight of what you have loved.

Let your bereavement be an offering to the gift of something meaningful, and when you're ready – not when you're told you should but when you've exhausted every tear and your heart can shatter no more – then you can move on and reclaim what you have left.

Additional meanings for the Five of Autumn Cups:

- complicated grief such as mourning someone you weren't allowed to grieve for
- choosing to sit in grief rather than bypass it
- feeling emotionally raw, tender, or cracked open
- watching others move on while you're still stuck in your moment of loss
- fixation on what's lost to the point of blindness.

Six of Autumn Cups

While this card typically represents nostalgia in autumn it becomes something deeper, leaning more into emotional inheritance. It's the ephemeral heirlooms shared such as traditions, songs, memories, or a scent that stirs up something buried, reminding you of a time long since passed.

After the immense grief of the Five of Autumn Cups, you can never predict when this card represents a blessing or a burden. Not all sojourns through the past are welcome: some are too painful to hold even when they remind you of something once loved, but it's your shared connections that give you legacy, for better or worse.

This card invites you to examine which legacies you wish to carry forward. You may have scripts that didn't originate with you or grief you've carried through your bones, or you're stuck in the past, reliving a version of events that cannot be restored. If that's the case it may be time to begin a journey toward healing, finally putting something to rest.

The past isn't always mournful. For some this card will be a blessing indeed, and represent a reconnection with something that once held great meaning. You might rekindle an ancestral tradition, return to a childhood passion, discover roots you didn't know you had, or extend an olive branch that restores a tarnished relationship.

Additional meanings for the Six of Autumn Cups:

- working through family of origin issues or ancestral trauma
- reparenting your inner child, especially around emotional safety, creativity, or cultural identity
- holding a hand-me-down object or heirloom and feeling more than you can explain
- living in the past or idolizing the way things used to be
- remembering where you came from and feeling proud.

Seven of Autumn Cups

The Seven of Autumn Cups asks you what you are afraid of committing to. A maiden is reading her tea leaves. She's already read six cups and now stares down at the seventh, hoping for yet another choice, each one more appealing than the last. She's now overwhelmed, wanting everything and choosing nothing.

The seasons keep turning even when you are paralyzed by your decisions. Eventually, autumn will turn to winter and the choices once offered will wither away. The appearance of this card is your sign that time is running out to make a choice. You may call it contemplating, reflecting, or processing when really you're just procrastinating.

Let this summons be an urgent call to examine what's holding you back. Scrutinize why potential and fantasy feel safer than solidifying a desire in reality: perhaps you do want it all but, deep down, something is pulling you more than others. Trust in where your heart is guiding you, and remember that something doesn't need to be perfect to feel right. Above all, know that not everything will wait for you and you may find yourself with a choice you didn't actually want.

Additional meanings for the Seven of Autumn Cups:

- chronic what if thinking that prevents forward movement
- shopping for spiritual tools or self-help methods but not engaging deeply with any of them
- letting yourself imagine alternate paths
- fear of regret, creating total paralysis
- keeping relationships or opportunities on hold just in case something better comes along.

Eight of Autumn Cups

The maiden has made her choice. Today claims her identity as a witch, leaving behind the only faith she's ever known. She hangs her cross necklace on a tree branch and walks away, a moment that is especially bittersweet as this cross meant something to her once upon a time. However, the religion she's practiced since childhood no longer supports her journey, and she finds herself in need of something different.

The Eight of Autumn Cups in the fall isn't a departure: it's a return, a soul retrieval where you can finally hear the wisdom of your own voice. It represents an awakening, bringing illumination to the ways you've left pieces of yourself behind every time you pleased, performed, or persisted when you wanted to let go. It's shedding an identity that's two sizes too small and walking a path that's an honest representation of who you are today.

This card's appearance in a reading is confirmation that seeking a new path is the right choice. Leaving behind such a large part of your life won't be easy, but holding on to the lie hasn't been either. However, this card doesn't invite rage or dramatic rejection. It invites reverence: for what once sustained you, and the courage it takes to now choose differently.

Additional meanings for the Eight of Autumn Cups:

+ healing from people pleasing, perfectionism, or persistent self-abandonment
+ trusting your inner compass, even when the path is unclear
+ avoiding confrontation by ghosting or emotionally disappearing
+ no longer pretending to believe in something for the sake of the comfort of others
+ choosing not to return to a toxic relationship, job, or habit you've romanticized.

Nine of Autumn Cups

The suit of Cups can feel like an emotional rollercoaster. Your heart sparked back to life with the Ace of Autumn Cups, it felt the raw ache of grief with the Five of Autumn Cups, and you walked away from something meaningful but out of place with the Eight of Autumn Cups. You've fought for this space of contentment with each breath and beat of your heart: every ritual, every heartbreak, every hard-earned ending, and now you're content to do nothing but show up for yourself and revel in your feeling of enoughness.

This card invites you to celebrate the life you've crafted, to acknowledge wishes come true not because a magical being granted it, but because you went out and made it happen. You've struggled along the way, but have also learned the power of being true to yourself. Your efforts have paid off.

The Nine of Autumn Cups isn't without its shadow. Humans are just as complex as decay dancing with the rich beauty of autumn. The person who made the wish isn't the person you are now, and what felt like a dream may not be all that it once appeared. Your desires may have shifted or you've reached this point only to realize it isn't actually enough. Be careful you aren't falling back into the old habits of the Seven of Autumn Cups, always seeking more instead of believing you have enough.

Additional meanings for the Nine of Autumn Cups:

- realizing you no longer need external approval to feel worthy
- finally believing you deserve rest, softness, or celebration after years of survival mode
- toasting yourself in solitude for something only *you* know you survived
- realizing a childhood wish has quietly come true, and you barely noticed
- feeling underwhelmed after getting what you thought you wanted.

Ten of Autumn Cups

The Ten of Autumn Cups invites you to reflect on the legacy of joy, to contemplate how your healing journey may serve as a map for others. The process of returning to yourself is for you, make no mistake about that, but what comes next is for those around you, for the people you unknowingly nurture by freeing yourself of old wounds. Each trauma healed is a cycle broken: one less person to project hurt onto. It's the children who won't know the sting of rejection for who they are or the future friends who can recognize you as one of their own because the light you shine is honest.

The traditional Ten of Cups has a tendency to represent happily ever after, and this is not that. The Ten of Autumn Cups is real, slowly shaped through the boundaries set, the vulnerabilities exposed, and the choices made to honor nascent connections. It's the house you've built that will be the house that builds others. It probably doesn't look like what you imagined when this all started. Perhaps you shifted from one identity to another or who you thought you would resonate with were drawn to an old version of you, but deep fulfillment has emerged despite all you've endured.

As ever, nothing lasts for a lifetime. The seasons shift, as is the natural order of life, and joy is fleeting, so enjoy this while you can. Don't justify happiness, loyalty, or resonance, and don't seek to find cracks in the walls or ghosts in the closet. Allow yourself this moment to be at peace and share in the joy of being seen.

Additional meanings for the Ten of Autumn Cups:

- blending families or beginning a new tradition that redefines home
- feeling emotionally secure after a long period of instability
- the importance of bonds that are chosen and nurtured rather than assigned
- settling into a new identity or chapter that aligns with who you've become
- celebrating a major relationship milestone: marriage, cohabitation, commitment ceremony.

Initiate of Autumn Cups

Like all of the initiates (or pages), this figure is starting a journey: not one of learning a skill or mental agility, but one of sensitivity, compassion, and understanding. The Initiate of Autumn Cups is a vessel for emotion, both theirs and those lingering in others that have gone unspoken. They feel the heaviness of what you're feeling often before you do. They cry during movies no one else finds sad, and they pick up on what isn't said in a room and carry it in their bones even if they don't understand its source.

In autumn, the most emotional season of them all, their gifts are heightened. The veil thins, and so does their protection. Ancestral grief, collective sorrow, and even the atmosphere of loss that permeates the season finds them and they hold it all. This evolutionary energy is not a card of mastery. The initiate is still learning how to sort through the mess: what's theirs and what's not, when to speak and when to hold back. Their emotions are unfiltered and unrefined. They may lash out, collapse inward, or withdraw completely as they learn to navigate the intense currents of their feelings. There's beauty in this rawness, but it's also volatile and overwhelming.

Still, this initiate is a gift. They are the ones who mourn what others dismiss, who feel for the forgotten, and who cry not only for themselves but for the world. Their path is one of radical sensitivity, of learning not to harden with time, and of understanding that being porous is a medicine and not a weakness when properly channeled.

Additional meanings for the Initiate of Autumn Cups:

- being emotionally raw, especially after a breakup, loss, or betrayal
- exploring what it means to be the emotional one in your family or friend group
- emotional immaturity in love, struggling to communicate needs clearly
- difficulty separating emotions from professional feedback or conflict
- beginning to explore psychic abilities or intuitive gifts.

Seeker of Autumn Cups

There's a longing stitched into the soul of this card, a yearning not for perfection but for something beautiful enough to believe in. This seeker is moved by emotion, led by instinct, and grounded in the melancholic truth that everything worthwhile eventually changes, yet still they search. They are not a wide-eyed dreamer chasing happily ever afters, nor are they naive to heartbreak. In fact, even though they've known enough disappointment to understand that devotion is a choice and not a guarantee, they continue to extend their cup. They continue to offer themselves up to the tenderness of being seen and the risk of being wrong, and they continue to follow their heart.

The Seeker of Autumn Cups reminds you that love – whether romantic, artistic, or spiritual – is a practice, that it isn't always fireworks and intensity. Often it's a quiet walk beside someone through a dark night, or the slow return to a creative project you thought had lost its value. There's a vulnerability to following what you love, especially when it doesn't come with a clear reward, which is so often the case.

This seeker, however, isn't interested in a prize: they follow for the poetry of the journey itself. Their presence in a reading invites you to romanticize the ordinary without losing sight of what's real and to devote yourself to what whispers your name, knowing it may be ephemeral but also knowing that the experience itself will shape you in ways perhaps permanence never could.

Additional meanings for the Seeker of Autumn Cups:

- a tendency to drift from one passion project to the next
- feeling drawn to someone artistic, sensitive, or emotionally complex
- spending driven by emotions or the desire to feel good: on romantic dinners, beautiful things, or indulgent experiences
- a need to be cautious of escapism through substances, fantasy, or emotionally driven eating
- a need for therapy, shadow work, or emotional vulnerability.

Shepherd of Autumn Cups

The Shepherd of Autumn Cups is the protector of emotional integrity. She is a sanctuary for the soft, the sensitive, and the misunderstood. Where the world rushes and demands performance, she invites depth, presence, and inner knowing. She sees what others overlook and recognizes the sacred in small, fleeting moments: an old photo, shared glance, or pot of tea on a rainy morning. Her power lies in discernment. She doesn't just feel deeply; she knows what to do with those feelings. She chooses her responses with care, speaks when it matters, and teaches that calm is not the absence of emotion but the mastery of it. When this card appears it's a sign you are being called to lead with your heart: not with sentimentality, but with emotional intelligence.

You may find yourself becoming a safe space for others or finally building one for yourself. This is emotional leadership: not through control or detachment, but through empathy, intuition, and the courage to stay soft in a hardening world.

Additional meanings for the Shepherd of Autumn Cups:

- careers involving therapy, healing arts, intuitive services, or creative direction
- learning to regulate your nervous system in the face of other people's emotions
- budgeting or investing for emotional security; for example, home, therapy, or healing retreats
- protecting your creative process by honoring your emotional cycles.

Keeper of Autumn Cups

Where the seeker and shepherd may weep or speak their sorrow, the keeper does not need to. He has mastered his emotions, reaching a maturity that doesn't always mean a confession. He is not withholding: he knows when to speak, when to witness, and when to hold space without asking for a single word.

In the season of autumn the keeper tends to the feelings you carry but cannot name. He walks beside the graves of emotions long buried, and decides what deserves resurrection and what can finally be laid to rest. You'll find him in small gestures such as lighting a candle for someone long gone, or the quiet act of setting a place at the table for a spirit no one else can see. He offers a new model of strength: one built not on stoicism, but on the right to have sacred privacy. His gift is not in how much he expresses, but in how deeply he feels without needing to be noticed for it. He is the ancestor who broke the chain of validation, the present-day elder who teaches emotional presence over performance.

Additional meanings for the Keeper of Autumn Cups:

- healing inherited emotional dynamics
- establishing inheritance or end-of-life financial plans with emotional clarity and love
- not reacting to every feeling, but creating space between stimulus and response
- learning to be comfortable in emotional depth without always needing closure.

Autumn Swords

Swords are traditionally linked with intellect, truth, and clarity, often representing mental struggles and breakthroughs. In autumn swords are replaced with branches to convey similar ideas through their connection with hard-earned growth, resilience, and the sharpness of nature's wisdom. Branches evoke imagery of bare trees in autumn and the harshness of learning to let go, emphasizing endings, persistence, and renewal. Finally, branches, like swords, can be strong yet vulnerable, representing the dual nature of intellect and truth.

Ace of Autumn Swords

The Ace of Autumn Swords marks the potential for mental liberation. It's the moment when truth downloads into your mind, unlocking clarity and deeper understanding. While the moment may land like a sudden flash of light in the darkness, the additional layer of autumn speaks of the past haunting your spirit. There is the sense that you've felt this in your bones long before it appeared in your mind. It's a sharp blade cutting through your denial, an inherited belief you can no longer hold or even an insight that shifts you in a meaningful way.

This is your chance to call the thing by its true name and move forward without delusion. What makes this moment so hard is that the next step after clarity is action. You could choose to ignore the information now in your possession and fall back into old habits, or you can claim your mental sovereignty and the things illusions have kept from you.

There is an urgency with all ace cards regardless of their suit or season. Autumn leaves will wither and fall whether you're ready or not, just as the truth this card represents won't linger forever. This is your summons to turn clarity into change before darkness descends upon you once again.

Additional meanings for the Ace of Autumn Swords:

- a suspicion is confirmed
- the moment you begin to write your own story
- something you've buried comes to the surface
- the beginning of mental maturity.

Autumn's wisdom

Download Whisper of Clarity Meditation at: seasonsofthewitchoracles.com/autumntarot.

Two of Autumn Swords

The Two of Autumn Swords appears when the clarity offered by the ace is met with indecision. A truth was presented to you, yet you believe you're caught between moving forward in clarity or pretending your situation is still obscured in mystery and doubt. The window of opportunity is swiftly closing and you must decide: it won't be long before you'll come face to face with the consequences of your inaction and find yourself standing in the sorrow of the Three of Autumn Swords.

You may believe you're protecting your heart from the dangers of fear, rejection, loss, or discomfort by ignoring the truth of what's before you, but your desire to protect is often a choice – perhaps unconscious – to delay the inevitable.

All is not lost as there's still potential. This pause could lead to illumination no matter how wrapped up in denial your choice may be. This card can mirror both The High Priestess if you use this moment to turn inward and listen to the nudges within your spirit, and The Hanged One if you allow this pause to become a genuine and deliberate moment to reflect rather than avoid what's ahead of you.

Additional meanings for the Two of Autumn Swords:

- detachment as a defense mechanism
- avoidance such as fear of opening a credit card bill
- a need to reconcile two different paths
- not listening to your inner knowing
- intentionally choosing mental fog.

Three of Autumn Swords

The grief of making a decision too late is the root of the Three of Autumn Swords. It represents the consequences of failing to act when it was within your power to do so. By choosing to avoid rather than confront you've been left with a very hard-earned lesson, one that cuts deeper because you saw it coming.

It's easy to get lost in a feeling of betrayal when you focus on the actions of others. You might understand your part in avoiding the impending doom but still struggle to reconcile the ways others have contributed to your pain. However, this isn't about them. This card doesn't appear to validate your heartbreak but to turn the focus back onto you and how you can take control of your recovery.

Allow this grief to become an initiation. Give purpose to this ache by choosing to let go of what is already gone. This is yet another chance at mental liberation, an opportunity to stop living in hindsight and start investing in a new chapter: one that embraces the hard lessons of your past and uses them to claim sovereignty over your future.

Additional meanings for the Three of Autumn Swords:

- a feeling of self-betrayal
- feeling a lack of closure
- the reopening of old wounds
- emotional exhaustion
- regret at not speaking up before someone passed.

Four of Autumn Swords

The suit of Autumn Swords gets off to a rocky start. You've faced hard truths (Ace of Autumn Swords), indecision (Two of Autumn Swords), and betrayal (Three of Autumn Swords). The Four of Autumn Swords represents what comes next: a reclamation of mental, emotional, and spiritual peace. This is the moment when you can go no further with all that you've carried, when you surrender to the exhaustion of pain, regret, and consequences.

Your body cannot heal without rest. Spring would not be possible without autumn's efforts to release and make space, nor can your heart become whole again while you're stuck in a loop of emotional survival. Being a suit of the mind, this card goes beyond rest and invites you to recalibrate the ways you'll move forward, to understand that lesson was learned but now you must give yourself pause to integrate it fully before charging on to the next season.

Additional meanings for the Four of Autumn Swords:

- recovery after hardship
- giving yourself time to grieve
- logging off social media to reset your mental health
- preserving your energy for what comes next
- taking a break from dating to reflect
- space to re-establish your own voice.

Five of Autumn Swords

There's a cost to getting your way when the Five of Autumn Swords appears. It suggests you've won a battle but lost something far more valuable in the process. A deeper way to view this card is a fracture of who you once were. You've abandoned a part of your integrity in order to survive and that survival has turned into self-preservation, which led to you becoming a permanent resident of fear.

When fear colors your actions it can lead to the expectation of a struggle, a constant brace for harm. You might weaponize your truth instead of firmly sharing your perspective, force boundaries through aggression rather than a healthy intention to protect your peace, or push a point that doesn't even matter in the name of reclaiming your voice.

It can also represent having not truly learned from the lessons of your past. Instead, you retreated back into a familiar pain that ultimately caused you to project hurt feelings onto others who didn't deserve your ire. What's left now is the king who's afraid of revenge lurking in every corner, or the captain who no longer has a team to lead. The Five of Autumn Swords doesn't ask whether you were right; it asks whether the cost was worth it. As it stands you may only be left with the ghost of a hollow victory.

Additional meanings for the Five of Autumn Swords:

- cruelty in the way you approached a situation
- alienating yourself in the name of winning
- a false sense of empowerment
- lashing out before others could hurt you
- micromanaging or undermining others
- burning bridges.

Six of Autumn Swords

Autumn is a liminal space that marks a transition, allowing you to immediately release and prepare for something new. The Six of Autumn Swords also stands in the in-between, representing the moment when you aren't fully healed but you aren't completely standing in grief either.

There's an openness to this card, the potential for so much possibility and, yes, that means there's also a fair amount of uncertainty. However, what you can know for certain is that you no longer fit in the space you came from. Maybe you've hurt yourself too many times by holding on too long, hoping things would change, or you're unable to fully heal while living in the midst of what continues to cause you pain. Perhaps you've hurt others and no amount of apology will ease the suffering, for them or for you.

There's nothing to be done for what was, but there's hope to be had in knowing the future can be vastly different from the past. There's a delicious sense of freedom in that alone. This departure isn't meant to be loud; there's no need for a dramatic declaration of intent, and you're not required to seek validation, praise, permission, or understanding. This departure isn't for anyone else but you as a way to honor your need for healing and peace.

Additional meanings for the Six of Autumn Swords:

- starting therapy after a traumatic event
- the beginning of a healing journey
- accepting the finality of a situation
- moving out of a toxic home or relationship
- learning you can love and leave at the same time
- embracing a liminal identity.

Seven of Autumn Swords

The easy interpretation for this card is deception or manipulation but it can go so much deeper than that. Perhaps the deception isn't what it seems: maybe what others view as duplicity is really cleverness as a means of survival, knowledge withheld when it didn't feel safe or reasonable to share, or isolation as a way to protect what you value most.

A witch hides her grimoire in the woods for fear of persecution. She hasn't done anything wrong yet some will view her as dangerous, something to be eradicated or contained. Thus she hides, she lies, and she bends the truth because her world wasn't built for her to thrive in.

Deceit can become discernment, a need to hold back when there's no clear evidence you're in a safe space. Secretiveness becomes strategy, where every move is considered and calculated. Perhaps your situation isn't as dire as the witch's, but that doesn't mean you owe your truth to anyone. Protect your right to hold secrets for yourself but, more than that, let this card serve as a summons for your rebellion. Never feel shame about breaking a rule that was never meant to serve you in the first place.

Additional meanings for the Seven of Autumn Swords:

- keeping a creative idea secret out of fear of theft
- downplaying something to avoid conflict
- hiding your beliefs or lifestyle for fear of rejection and shame
- thinking ahead of everyone else
- code switching or filtering the truth.

Eight of Autumn Swords

The Eight of Autumn Swords is a mental cage, one your mind crafted to help you believe the stories you've inherited from other sources. There's often a small kernel of truth to these tales, making it even easier to cage you in, but it's a distorted truth at best. It whispers things like: *I'm not good enough. I'm asking for too much. I don't deserve this. I'm not ready.* Once the words take hold fear is more than happy to fill in the blanks. What started as a small seed of doubt has transformed into a full prison of anxiety, leaving you disoriented and believing there's no escape.

The maiden is trapped inside a mausoleum. She can either wither away turning this cage into a spiritual coffin, or she can leave these stories behind so they can die instead. At its root this card is a reminder that you aren't weak or lost: you're conditioned. All is not adrift, as this card has appeared to illuminate the path to freedom and to remind you that while the prison you're in may be real, you're also the key to your salvation.

Additional meanings for the Eight of Autumn Swords:

- being paralyzed by impostor syndrome
- conditioned self-doubt
- feelings of overwhelm
- discrediting intuitive hits
- a narrowed perception of your reality.

Nine of Autumn Swords

If one word could sum up the Nine of Autumn Swords it would be *haunting*. This is when your mind becomes a form of self-violence, turning all your fears, anxieties, panic, grief, shame, and vulnerability into ghosts that descend on you at once. It's the sleepless nights spent rehearsing disasters, and the dread creeping up your spine convincing you something terrible is about to happen even though you have no evidence to support the fear.

The Nine of Autumn Swords hasn't appeared to deny your feelings, but it does challenge your perception of them. Just because someone else can't see a ghost doesn't mean it isn't there. The danger still feels real to you, but the key is knowing that feeling isn't always fact and that what you're imagining is your mind's way of protecting you after a long time of past hurt and regret.

This card marks the breaking point in the spiral of self-cruelty and to offer you a light in the darkness, urging you to seek safety. Be it through therapy, your community, more productive rest, or ritual, the medicine you need now isn't more thought: compassion and support are your lifelines. You don't have to live inside a battlefield in your mind, not if you don't want to.

Additional meanings for the Nine of Autumn Swords:

+ the haunting of "What if?"
+ anxiety attacks
+ living with PTSD, complex trauma, or hypochondria
+ a crisis of conscience
+ replaying past mistakes in your head for hours.

Ten of Autumn Swords

There's nothing left to support an attachment when the Ten of Autumn Swords appear. This is the final leaf falling from the tree before winter sets in, the losses that can't be reclaimed and the acceptance that you've poured everything you have into saving a situation but you haven't a single drop left to give. This ending is painful. You may feel a sense of failure, deep regret, or mournful sadness over the loss of what once held so much potential. It may even feel as though you can't go on after such a devastating blow.

The Ten of Autumn Swords doesn't sugarcoat the gravity of your circumstances: there's tragedy in your situation to be sure but there's also hope, however small it may appear. A flower doesn't die because it loses its leaves and petals. Tiny seeds fall to the earth that will be covered in soil, snow, storm, and stillness, yet they'll survive and bloom come spring.

This defeat is only a temporary setback. This card appears to encourage you to hold on to the seeds of tomorrow. Lingering in your grief will do nothing to change the outcome, nor will spinning a narrative of you as the victim. What you're grieving may have you for a time, but now it just represents a dark chapter. Every chapter ends, however, and you're still the author of your next story.

Additional meanings for the Ten of Autumn Swords:

+ a feeling of hitting rock bottom
+ experiencing a crisis that forces you to start over
+ the full collapse of a belief system, identity, or lifestyle
+ a crash after running on empty for far too long
+ complete loss of trust in a person or situation.

Initiate of Autumn Swords

The Initiate of Autumn Swords reflects a moment of mental emergence, when you begin to think for yourself, examine your beliefs, and question the ideas that were once handed to you without consent. This card often appears when you're just beginning to reclaim your mind as your own and learning to trust your voice as your source of truth.

However, the initiate hasn't developed the maturity to wield that truth just yet. They may react too quickly, cutting with newfound clarity that wounds more than it should. This can manifest in overcorrection: becoming argumentative or overly skeptical, or an addiction to being right. It can just as easily signal a hunger to read, research, and challenge outdated systems, especially when they conflict with your evolving values.

As an evolutionary energy this card appears when you're forming opinions but haven't lived through them enough to test, and that's okay. This is your sign to try on perspectives, to fumble your way through conversations and witness where your mind clashes with your conditioning.

The Initiate of Autumn Swords isn't just about learning, it's about mental liberation: the ability to name the beliefs that were never yours to begin with, and to begin curating an inner world that actually reflects who you are becoming.

Additional meanings for the Initiate of Autumn Swords:

- a tendency to speak before thinking: watch for defensiveness or performative intelligence
- reading books on social justice, gender, or philosophy and realizing your worldview is shifting
- reading too much into texts, tone, or body language
- asking bold questions in financial conversations
- feeling pressure to sound smart or overcompensate because you're the new one on the team.

Seeker of Autumn Swords

This seeker represents urgency. They are rushing toward a goal with wind-whipped hair and razor-sharp thoughts. They draw their sword, ready to cut before finding a threat. Their mind is always churning with analysis, insight, and internal dialogue. They're brilliant but moving too fast, and their energy is too raw right now at this unchecked speed.

In autumn the world naturally begins to slow down, but the seeker forgets to also slow down. Their mind is still trying to outthink everyone around them. This is challenging enough for others, but for the seeker the challenge is that their thoughts are moving faster than they can feel them.

This card appears when you're sprinting toward a solution with no map. It represents someone who speaks before thinking, commits before planning, or creates before processing, all in an effort to appear complex. The Seeker of Autumn Swords urges you to recognize when action is simply masked avoidance. Sometimes you aren't thinking clearly, you're spiraling, intellectualizing, and reacting from panic. That's not clarity, nor is it honest.

Additional meanings for the Seeker of Autumn Swords:

- making impulsive purchases to relieve mental stress, then feeling regret later
- over-intellectualizing your spiritual practice: reading everything but integrating little
- struggling with obsessive thought patterns, over-analysis, or catastrophizing
- becoming fixated on needing to know what someone is thinking at all times.

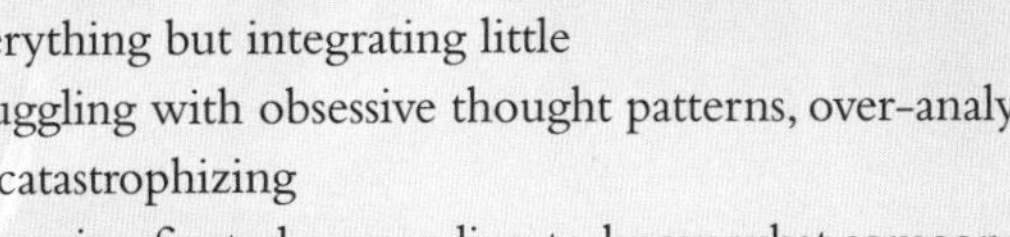

Shepherd of Autumn Swords

The Shepherd of Autumn Swords is the protector of inner truth. She isn't cold because she has no feelings: she simply understands that not everyone deserves access to her deepest thoughts and emotions, or even the shallow ones for that matter. Nor does she view her emotions as weaknesses. What sets her apart is her strategy: she doesn't let her feelings control her, but she doesn't deny them either. She understands that emotional clarity often requires distance and that boundaries are a form of love: not just for others, but for herself.

As an evolutionary energy you're being asked to examine your question with a calm, clear eye, to rise above reactive behavior and, instead, study your emotions and then respond with insight. How are you giving your power away? In what ways do you contort your truth to conform to others'? What situations have you entered into without having the full story?

Learn to make peace with silence in a world that is too quick to talk before listening. The shepherd's words may be few, but when she speaks they matter. Her love may be guarded, but it's deeply loyal to those who have earned her loyalty. Her presence in a reading reminds you that you don't owe access to anyone who hasn't proven they can hold it with care. You are allowed to be exacting, even if it makes others uncomfortable.

Additional meanings for the Shepherd of Autumn Swords:

- learning to love from a place of self-respect, not self-sacrifice
- making financial decisions with your future self in mind, not from temporary emotional states
- being asked by spirit to become more selective about what you give your energy to
- a career in strategy, law, writing, or research
- choosing peace over companionship.

Keeper of Autumn Swords

There comes a time when the discussion ends. When all opinions have been heard and all facts considered, it's time to make the call. The Keeper of Autumn Swords appears in these moments to bring clarity to ambiguity. He is the embodiment of hard-won wisdom, the one who listened, questioned, investigated, and observed. Now, with cool resolve, he speaks the final word. He doesn't waver or second-guess because he's allowed himself the proper time to examine all angles in private. You may see him as cold, distant, or arrogant when his true gift is honesty.

The keeper understands that some truths aren't kind but are still necessary. Some boundaries will upset others, yet they must be held. Some consequences will be painful, but nevertheless they must come to pass. The keeper isn't interested in emotional excuses or hopes or fears; he's only concerned with what *is*.

When this card appears you may be facing a decision or verdict that requires clarity, not comfort. You may also be called to take the lead on your situation: to mediate, instruct, defend, or declare. It could also mean someone in your life is holding authority that affects you, and you must learn how to navigate their rules without losing yourself.

The shadow expression of this card lies in emotional detachment. The keeper can become so devoted to logic that he forgets compassion. He may assume he knows best and silence other voices that offer nuance. Ask yourself whether you are being guided by clarity or control. Despite its dark side this card is a blessing when you need structure as it tells you there *is* an answer. It just might not be the one you hoped for, but it will set you free.

Additional meanings for the Keeper of Autumn Swords:

+ an impartial, emotionless leader who makes hard calls based on reason and precedent
+ having a partner who intellectualizes their feelings and may struggle with emotional vulnerability
+ cutting off someone financially due to their repeated misuse of support
+ receiving a firm diagnosis and needing to follow a structured, possibly strict treatment plan.

Autumn Pentacles

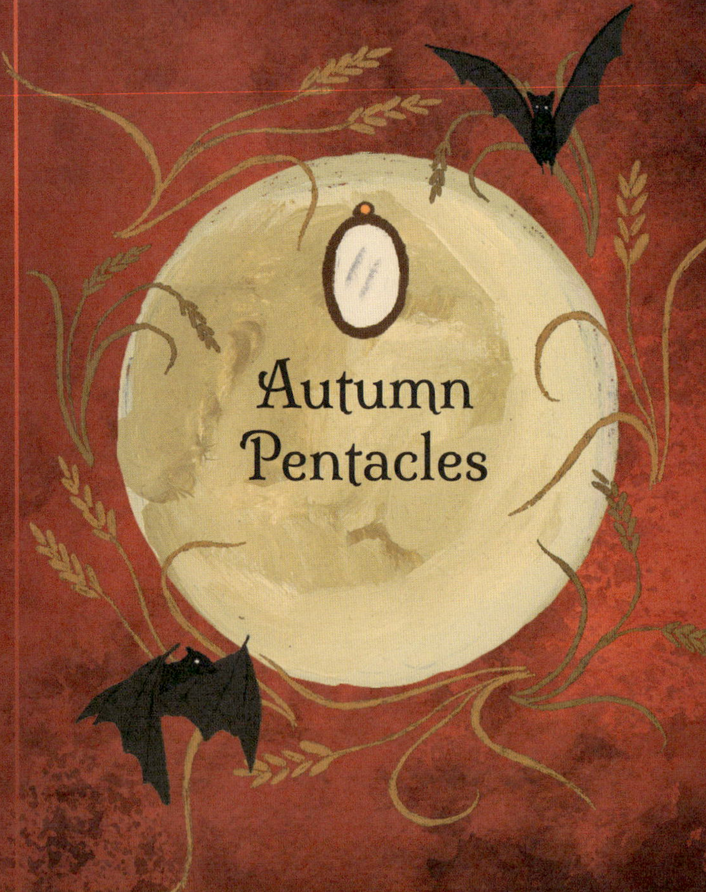

Mirrors are the symbol of pentacles in *Autumn Tarot*. Traditionally, the suit of Pentacles is associated with material wealth, career, physicality, and grounding. Mirrors, however, shift the focus to self-worth, personal value, and self-reflection, and the interplay between inner and outer worlds. This aligns beautifully with the introspective and transitional energy of autumn, as it encourages you to examine your relationship with the material and how it reflects your inner state. Throughout this suit many of the interpretations have been written from the perspective of discovering your self-worth, but should you feel as though this is too much to confront in this season, simply replace value with external accomplishments.

Ace of Autumn Pentacles

Like all aces, the Ace of Autumn Pentacles is a seed of potential. It's an idea, nascent feeling or opportunity for advancement. It's the promise of personal worth: still unproven, yet alive within you and waiting to be claimed.

A young maiden buries a mirror, representing how she sees herself now, with quiet faith in who she'll one day become: not out of shame or because she feels small, but because she knows there's a bigger purpose for her lurking within her bones.

Throughout the suit of Pentacles she'll envision, gather, and labor then fail, try again, and master, each time growing her self-belief, skills, and capacity to receive. This is not because she's broken, but because worth is something you learn to hold through consistent action.

The challenge is that this is only the beginning and her potential is not yet embodied. There's still so much work to do, for while she feels the promise of a greater destiny she must show up for herself again and again. She must redefine her identity to match what she's asking for. The Ace of Autumn Pentacles doesn't offer a guarantee; it asks whether you're willing to become the kind of person who can hold the dreams you see for yourself.

Additional meanings for the Ace of Autumn Pentacles:

- applying for a job you're not sure you deserve yet
- starting a side hustle, fitness routine, or healing regime, or getting a makeover
- a new project or routine that may not feel glamorous but has real staying power
- planting something that will not bloom until spring
- starting things you never allow yourself to finish due to feeling unworthy.

Two of Autumn Pentacles

A maiden holds two different mirrors. In one she sees herself as confident, valuable, and deserving of respect, while in the other she only sees cracks in her exterior. She sees someone who's inexperienced, insecure, lacking resources, and posing as something more: her sense of worth shifting in response to external circumstances. She's managing this teetering of emotions for now, but at some point one of these mirrors will overtake the other and a story – for better or worse – will become her truth.

The Two of Autumn Pentacles reflects the fragility of building an identity or immovable expectation on ever-changing circumstances. Perhaps you feel the need to prove yourself through productivity, or your confidence hinges on how much you're able to meet obligations you never consciously agreed to.

It's easy to feel as though you have it under control when life is at ease, but will you manage when the wind blows too hard and the rain begins to fall? Knowing your center, your true worth, what's most important, and your non-negotiables can help you maintain a better sense of equilibrium. This card extends beyond the autumn lens of self-value and can just as easily speak to balancing priorities of family, work, personal endeavors, and obligations. It reminds you that balance isn't about doing it all, it's about prioritizing what matters most and allowing space for change. Priorities evolve, which means you can too. Let your reflection shift without losing sight of who you are at your center.

Additional meanings for the Two of Autumn Pentacles:

- giving more than you're receiving
- people pleasing disguised as multitasking
- juggling multiple jobs or income streams
- living in survival mode without ever feeling grounded or settled
- trying to hold multiple expressions at once: joy and grief, clarity and doubt, readiness and fear.

Three of Autumn Pentacles

Developing worth is an inside journey, yet it never built in isolation. Those around you will help shape the way you view yourself. This card brings light to the people who walk beside you: those who challenge you to see yourself as worthy, support you through doubt and uncertainty, or share in the quiet act of building something that matters.

In the autumnal context this card represents how individual harvests feed the collective. Your value is reflected in what you do for yourself but also in how you show up for others, contributing to their worth as well. You are a part of something greater than yourself when this card appears: you belong to a lineage of friends and co-creators, family, and ancestors past, each leaving an imprint on the identity that is shaping yourself today and the future to come. Some will keep the mirror polished while others will simply witness and confirm the beauty of the reflection upon its surface, but all of them matter.

It can be scary and make you feel vulnerable to be seen mid-process. It might feel safer to wait until your identity or idea is polished and perfect, but perfection is a myth. A mirror of value built together will remind you that confidence and worth shared is much more powerful. You do not need to hold your vision alone, nor are you supposed to. There is strength in letting others contribute to your unfolding story and in you contributing to theirs.

Additional meanings for the Three of Autumn Pentacles:

+ blending ideas without losing your voice
+ joining a coven, collective, or spiritual cohort where you're both student and teacher
+ a need to align values, goals, and communication styles to avoid future obstacles
+ receiving feedback through praise, correction, or perspective and using it for positive evolution
+ struggling to feel seen in a team setting despite making vital contributions.

Four of Autumn Pentacles

A maiden is utterly obsessed with putting her best face forward: she never wants anyone to see how she looks underneath all of the hair, make-up, and clothes. She has four mirrors in front of her to check each and every angle before putting one foot out the door. Her curated appearance is her armor, and she's clutching tightly to it to feel safe. She believes removing this persona will result in the withdrawal of affection, resources, trust, or connection from others so she polishes, she perfects, and she controls, all in an effort to hold on to what she believes she cannot live without.

The traditional Four of Pentacles represents scarcity and the fear of losing what you've achieved or gained, especially when it comes to money or career. When you filter this idea through the lens of Autumn Pentacles, or internal value, what's being hoarded out of fear isn't money or power: it's authenticity, and it's the right to be *enough* just as you are without performance for love or respect.

When this card appears it invites you to examine how you're holding on too tightly, be it in the realm of prosperity, your relationships, or anything else that is not fully within your control. Often this card is a sign that your position is much more stable than you've let yourself believe. There's no need to pinch or perform in an effort to ensure your security. However, the tighter you clutch the more you drive others away. Be mindful that your efforts to protect yourself do not become a self-fulfilling prophecy.

Additional meanings for the Four of Autumn Pentacles:

- hyper-control as a trauma response
- withholding affection, vulnerability, or personal truths in a relationship from fear that the real you will be rejected
- being afraid that if you rest, loosen control, or shift direction then everything you've built will fall apart
- hoarding resources or opportunities from fear there won't be enough left for you
- resisting change because you are afraid of instability.

Five of Autumn Pentacles

The Five of Autumn Pentacles reflects the feeling of being discarded, undervalued, deeply unseen, or ignored: by a person, community, or even by your own sense of self. This card goes far beyond material lack, landing in the realm of spiritual and emotional scarcity. It's easy to pull this card and see it as confirmation that you do not have enough resources, time, love, or respect, although this isn't meant to validate your fears but rather to show you how deeply rooted your mindset is in feelings of unworthiness and lack.

When this card appears you may be asking: do I still matter if I no longer have anything to offer? Am I still desirable if I'm so depleted I don't even feel like a whole person? Shame takes hold when this card appears, not because you're unworthy but because you've mistaken feeling alone for being unwanted.

Perhaps you have walked your path in loneliness for so long you've forgotten how to ask for help, and now you believe help is no longer available. This couldn't be further from the truth. Yes, your situation is hard, but it needn't be a lasting blow if you can put aside your pride and seek assistance. Even now in your most depleted state you are still worthy of warmth, support, and care. The hardest part may be letting yourself believe that.

Additional meanings for the Five of Autumn Pentacles:

- self-exile due to shame or guilt
- belief that you're always behind
- experiencing financial instability that's triggering deeper questions about self-worth
- experiencing a crisis of faith: feeling as though your guides, intuition, or higher self has gone quiet
- questioning if you'll ever get back to the version of yourself who felt whole
- unhealed wounds around abandonment.

Six of Autumn Pentacles

It's truly remarkable how a modern society built on seeking "more" can have such trouble learning to receive with apology or shame. Through the energy of autumn the Six of Autumn Pentacles challenges the conditioning of chronic independence and over-functioning. It reminds you that seeking support is not a failure, it's an inevitability you will face many times throughout your journey, as does everyone else.

This card may appear when support is being offered to you but you are struggling to accept it as a genuine gift. It is not a burden to need help, nor does it diminish your value. You are simply in a season of acceptance, allowing what is given freely and without expectation to be the blessing that it is.

At some point you will find yourself in the position of sharing with others, a position that may not be possible without the help of others. The exchange of resources is an endless circle: you give, you receive, and you give again. At its heart this card represents generosity and becomes a sacred reflection of support rather than a transaction of shame.

Additional meanings for the Six of Autumn Pentacles:

- struggling to charge appropriately for your work
- a friend or partner offering support and your first instinct is to decline, even though you need it
- becoming the one in need after always being the strong one
- taking on healing roles such as coach, reader, or guide and learning not to overgive to prove your worth
- feeling resentful in a job or partnership where you give more than you receive
- overextending yourself financially, emotionally, or energetically.

Seven of Autumn Pentacles

A maiden walks through a hallway of mirrors, each one representing a decision she's made. She's evaluating her choices to see whether they are truly based on her own values and desires, or if she's making decisions based on what she thinks others want or what she believes makes her more desirable.

The Seven of Autumn Pentacles reflects a moment of deep inner inventory. It invites you to answer a simple question: have your choices supported your desires? You may feel disoriented or full of doubt and wondering if you should continue at all, but this card isn't meant to be a moment of failure, only an opportunity to clarify your path.

Each journey needs a period of reflection, a chance to see what's working and what is not. If you find that your choices have led you to the wrong place, then accept this truth with grace and adjust your path moving forward. If instead you're operating in a way that brings you joy, pride, and fulfillment, then continue as you have been. There's no need for harsh judgment or beratement, only a willingness to evaluate and act accordingly.

Additional meanings for the Seven of Autumn Pentacles:

- feeling stuck or stalled in a business or career even though consistent effort is being made
- taking a step back to ask: *who am I becoming, and do I actually want to become that person?*
- trying to make it work with someone but realizing the effort is one-sided
- wondering if it's too late to pivot, start over, or reimagine your life
- questioning whether you've spent years chasing the wrong dream, persona, or relationship
- awakening to how much of your life has been built around seeking approval, not fulfillment.

Eight of Autumn Pentacles

At its heart the Eight of Autumn Pentacles represents repetition for the purpose of mastery. It speaks to the process of devotion and a willingness to do the often-unseen labor required to truly excel in your craft. Through the energy of autumn this card becomes less about the task itself and more about who you're becoming as a result of your efforts. Whether it's spiritual practice, a career path, creative work, or building a strong sense of personal value, you're not just doing the thing: the thing is shaping *you*.

What you repeat becomes who you are. If you speak to yourself with sureness and confidence, then in time you will become a sure and confident person. If you paint every day, then one day you will find you are an artist. Mastery of any skill is not something given without training or practice, just as self-worth is not given to you without your consistent commitment to showing up for yourself. You come closer and closer to your goal with each brush stroke or reframe of an outdated belief.

When this card appears it's to remind you to put in the work, to stop seeking transformation by magic and start putting in the effort to become who you desire to be. It also speaks to the necessity for patience and a willingness to make mistakes. There's a need to release perfectionism when this card arrives, choosing progress instead.

Additional meanings for the Eight of Autumn Pentacles:

- practicing a craft such as writing, tarot, herbalism, or design daily and beginning to see the evolution
- undoing years of self-criticism through repeated acts of self-compassion and accountability
- rebuilding trust with a partner, friend, or family member through small, intentional choices over time
- quiet consistency that doesn't generate praise, applause, or external validation.

Nine of Autumn Pentacles

The Nine of Autumn Pentacles is a card of luxury, of being able to say: *"I've done it. I've made it."* It's an invitation not just to claim the rewards of your hard-earned success, but to indulge in them and embody a feeling of accomplishment. The image reflects a woman wearing a necklace of nine mirrors as a representation of her hard-earned value. She no longer absorbs the criticisms and objections of her actions given to her by others. Harsh words bounce off the mirrors and return to their source, allowing the owner to feel the ugliness of their words.

In autumn the traditional Nine of Pentacles shifts slightly to the luxury of no longer needing validation. You've journeyed through the suit of Pentacles, reclaiming your worth through hardship and healing, and now you can luxuriate in the feeling of being enough.

There is a certain level of confidence that will naturally settle over your spirit when you reach a higher level of success, be it internal or external. It's rooted in the acknowledgment that you set a goal and made it happen. There's no longer a need to prove or perform: you are what you set out to become. When this card appears it's a gentle reminder to enjoy what you've worked so hard to achieve. The hardest part is behind you now, so there's no need to question what you can do because you can see it for yourself.

Additional meanings for the Nine of Autumn Pentacles:

- enjoying financial independence after a long period of hustle or instability
- recognizing that being single, solo, or selective is a luxury, not a failure
- creating your own definition of success, and actually living it
- choosing stillness and savoring as a form of embodied wisdom and self-care.

Ten of Autumn Pentacles

Of all the tens, the Ten of Autumn Pentacles represents contentment: not with money or anything physical, but a life of owning worth and love and purpose. There's no longer a need to be seen by others to feel beautiful or worthy. Here the maiden sees herself. She's enough; in fact, she's more than enough and she holds her satisfaction with life as her most precious possession.

This card represents a feeling of fullness. It appears when you have much to be thankful for, traditionally when it comes to wealth and status but also emotional, spiritual, and personal fulfillment. You've traveled through the suit – through fear and effort, through isolation and connection, and through rebuilding –

and now you have arrived in a safe space where your values, work, and sense of self are all in alignment.

This is not the end of a journey, but it is the end of a chapter. It's a moment to pause and honor how far you've come before moving on to your next adventure. Rest here, taking ample time to express and, more importantly, to feel your gratitude. Reflect upon all you've done, and trust that what you've built is enough to shelter you in joy for many more seasons to come.

Additional meanings for the Ten of Autumn Pentacles:

- becoming a steward of all you have built
- closing a chapter of ambition and finally moving into a season of refinement instead of striving
- choosing not to pass down harmful beliefs about money, gender roles, or emotional expression to the next generation
- a long-standing friendship or marriage entering a new phase.

Initiate of Autumn Pentacles

The Initiate of Autumn Pentacles represents your willingness to become someone new, especially when it comes to career, finances, or self-worth. It means to begin again, but in real, aligned practice rather than theory. The initiate marks the first day of showing up for yourself, the early, unsteady steps of learning to live in integrity with what you say you want.

The initiate isn't seeking to impress. She's patient, honest, and thorough: shortcuts simply won't do for what she has planned. Her strength lies in her willingness to be seen as a beginner, in willing to do the small, slow, often unglamorous work that self-mastery requires.

When this card appears it could signal a sign to start a new project, rebuild after a loss, return to your body, or redefine your sense of worth. This card represents a "Yes" and urges you to begin, but to do so with slow, deliberate action. Speed is not the goal when this card arrives: integrity is. You will have moments when doubt creeps in, and that isn't a sign to give up but a sign to disengage your sense of value from perfection.

Additional meanings for the Initiate of Autumn Pentacles:

+ a student mindset: being in the process of learning, researching, or preparing
+ self-sabotage through inaction or constant research without execution
+ realizing that you don't have to have it all figured out to be worthy of love
+ learning to cook or eat differently to support your energy and long-term well-being
+ choosing longer, slower travel over rushed itineraries.

Seeker of Autumn Pentacles

The Seeker of Autumn Pentacles represents commitment to your chosen path. This is where action starts to stitch itself into your spirit, where your choices reflect your values and especially when no one's watching. The seeker shows up: they prepare the soil, they tend the body, and they budget, stretch, rest, and repeat. They're not chasing results, they're practicing what it means to be in alignment and what it means to devote themselves to something and stick to those boundaries.

There is great strength in this steadiness. Like the initiate, the seeker is not here to impress: they're here to do something that lasts. Their worth isn't measured in how loud they can be or how much space they take up, but in *integrity*, in how consistently they return to the work, practice, and promises they've made to themselves.

This card reminds you there will be times when progress feels invisible or stalled and when the pace feels achingly slow, but the seeker knows that in the rhythm of autumn slowness is sacred. Nothing rushed lasts, and nothing ignored thrives. Everything worthwhile is built in layers, and the seeker is happy to wait for excellence to unfold.

Pulling this card means you're being asked to commit, recommit, or simply stay the course. Things may appear dull or even non-existent, but that doesn't mean nothing is happening. Keep going, even when no one claps. Maybe especially then.

Additional meanings for the Seeker of Autumn Pentacles:

- sticking to a budget or investment plan even when you're tempted to deviate
- building tolerance for boredom, repetition, or slowness
- showing up for a partner in small but meaningful ways
- doing the thing you said you'd do, even when it's inconvenient
- running a business with integrity rather than speed or for quick profit.

Shepherd of Autumn Pentacles

The Shepherd of Autumn Pentacles is the protector of everything you've earned, not by luck but through consistent effort. Like all Pentacle court cards, this shepherd has overcome the need to perform her value for others. She no longer overextends herself, choosing deep self-respect, personal care, and precise, intentional action.

Her magic lives in the tangible: the way she prepares food, balances her schedule, waters her plants, and most importantly says "No" without guilt. She is the high priestess of daily devotion, turning ordinary habits into sacred rituals. She knows that taking care of what she loves is never small, it's the foundation everything else rests on.

This card arrives when you're being asked to hold and nourish what you've built: not just the external wins, but the rhythms and rituals that support your everyday well-being. It also reminds you that tending to your needs is not an act of indulgence, it's a self-responsibility, because when you are well everything around you will also grow stronger. You have the strength and peace to support your community without unraveling at your own seams. This card isn't about hustling more or being a superhuman, it's about taking care of what matters most and that includes you.

Additional meanings for the Shepherd of Autumn Pentacles:

- someone with grounded wisdom and nurturing presence playing a key role in your situation
- moving away from overgiving and into right-sized care
- prioritizing quality over quantity in your purchases
- releasing people-pleasing tendencies and choosing sustainable intimacy
- mothering yourself so you don't parent your partner
- slowing down enough to notice where you're thriving and where you're leaking energy.

Keeper of Autumn Pentacles

The Keeper of Autumn Pentacles represents embodied value. She's worked hard over the journey of Pentacles, and that effort has created a grounded being who knows how to receive, how to protect what she values most and, most importantly, how to pass it on to others. This master is a legacy holder: of wealth and achievement, yes, but also of standards and personal worth. She's the example to model yourself on because she knows what it means to be a leader. She has integrity, generosity, stewardship, patience, and fortitude.

She doesn't need to broadcast her accomplishments because her life is her message. Her actions speak louder than words ever could. The way she moves through her home, body, and relationships mean they all become teachable moments.

This card arrives when you're being asked to root into your own authority. What are you teaching, consciously or not, through how you show up in the world? Are you living in alignment with your values or simply aspiring to them? Whether you're building a home, running a business, leading a family, or holding space for a friend, the keeper reminds you that leadership doesn't always look like being in command. Sometimes it looks like consistency. Sometimes it looks like *care* and, yes, sometimes it looks like tough love. The key is knowing what needs to show up and where.

Additionally, this card reminds you that wealth, accomplishment, and personal value mean nothing if it ends with you: share what you've learned with others, learn how to be a guide for those around you, and live your life as though you're building something that outlasts it.

Additional meanings for the Keeper of Autumn Pentacles:

- a figure of stability, support, or generosity entering your life
- becoming the financial anchor in a household or family
- mentoring others in healthy boundaries, rituals, or communication
- no longer improvising and building systems that serve your future self
- developing wealth consciousness by embodying wealth rather than chasing it.

The hidden path

Your journey with this deck doesn't end here, as additional reflections, hidden wisdom, and unexpected layers await those who know where to look. If you've made it this far, trust that there is more. Step beyond the veil and continue the work at: seasonsofthewitchoracles.com/autumntarot.

About the author

Lorriane Anderson is a bestselling author, spiritual teacher, and internationally recognized tarot and oracle expert. She views the seasons, sabbats, moon phases, and natural cycles as portals for personal growth and deep soul remembrance. Her work blends grounded earth wisdom with celestial insight, guiding others to develop a more intuitive and meaningful connection with themselves and the world around them.

Lorriane is the creator of numerous beloved books and decks including the *Seasons of the Witch* oracle series, which has become a staple in the modern mystic's collection. Her work has been featured in *Oprah Daily*, *The Spruce*, *Reader's Digest*, *Kindred Spirit*, *VoyageLA*, and *The Daily Star*, among others.

Lorriane currently resides in Los Angeles, California, where she continues to create tools for seekers, seers, and soulful practitioners across the globe.

spiritelement.co | **seasonsofthewitchoracles.com/autumntarot**
@spiritelement

About the illustrator

Tijana Lukovic is an illustrator based in the small medieval city of Gent in Belgium. Her paintings and illustrations are inspired by the magical and metaphysical realms, containing traces of folklore, fairytale, mythology, and love for nature. Previous works include the Seasons of the Witch Imbolc, Litha, Lammas, Ostara, and Mabon oracle decks published by Rockpool Publishing.

tijanadraws.com
@tijanadraws